GRAPHIC LIBRARY

GRAPHIC SCIENCE

THE ILLUMINATING WORLD OF LIGHT WITH MAX AXIOM SUPER SCIENTIST

by Emily Sohn
illustrated by Nick Derington

Consultant:
Leslie Flynn, PhD
Science Education, Chemistry
University of Minnesota

Capstone press
Mankato, Minnesota

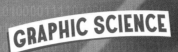

Graphic Library is published by Capstone Press,
151 Good Counsel Drive, P.O. Box 669, Mankato, Minnesota 56002.
www.capstonepress.com

Printed in the United States of America

1 2 3 4 5 6 12 11 10 09 08 07

Library of Congress Cataloging-in-Publication Data
Sohn, Emily.
The illuminating world of light with Max Axiom, super scientist / by Emily Sohn; illustrated by Nick Derington.
p. cm.—(Graphic library. Graphic science)
Summary: "In graphic novel format, follows the adventures of Max Axiom as he explains the science behind light"—Provided by publisher.
Includes bibliographical references and index.
ISBN-13: 978-1-4296-0140-5 (hardcover)
ISBN-10: 1-4296-0140-X (hardcover)
1. Light—Juvenile literature. 2. Adventure stories—Juvenile literature. I. Derington, Nick, ill. II. Title. III. Series.
QC360.S645 2008
535—dc22 2007002264

Art Director and Designer
Bob Lentz

Cover Artist
Tod Smith

Editor
Christopher L. Harbo

Photo illustration credits: iStockphoto, 23; Shutterstock/Jo-Hanna Wienert, 13

TABLE of CONTENTS

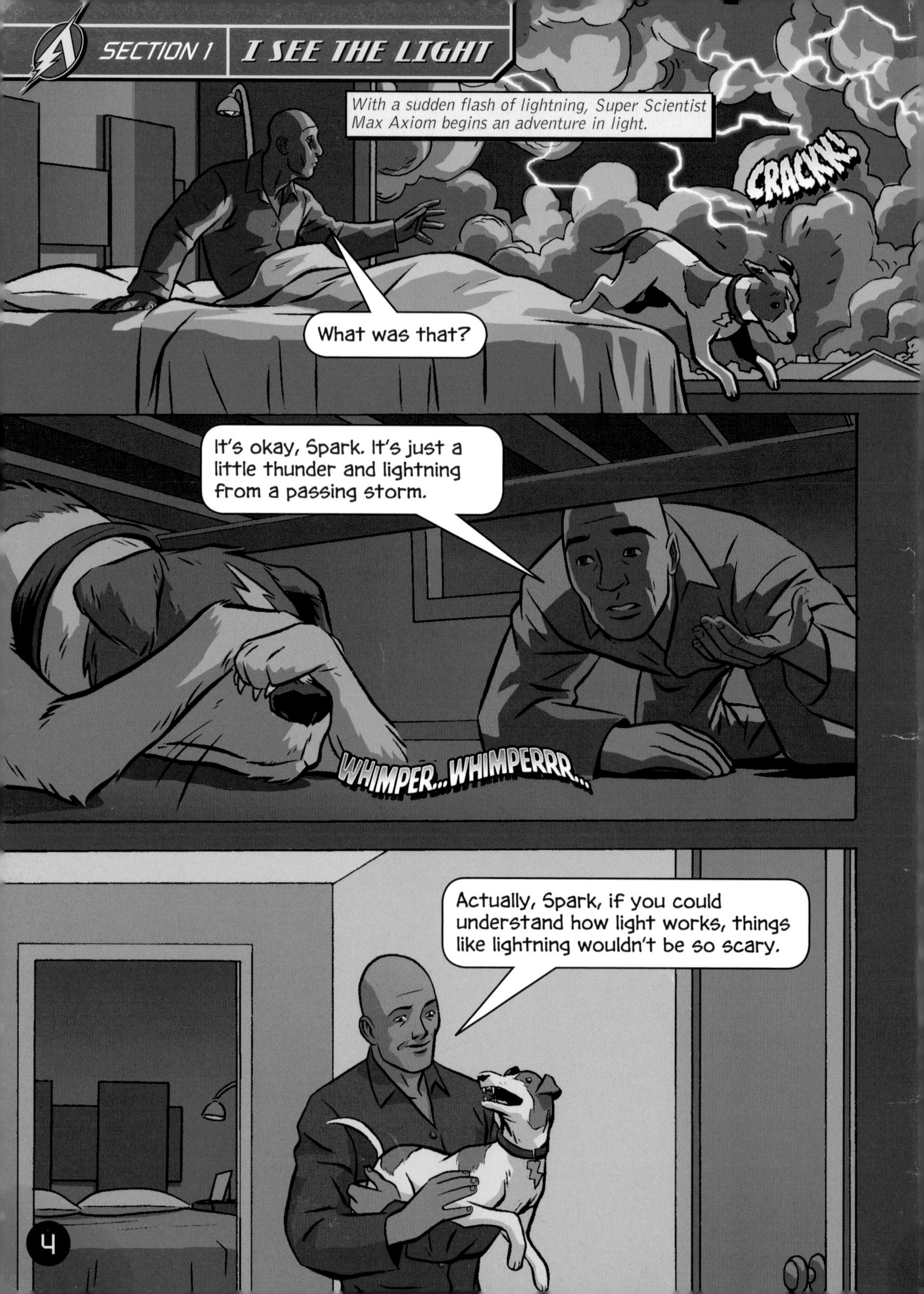
SECTION 1
I SEE THE LIGHT
With a sudden flash of lightning, Super Scientist Max Axiom begins an adventure in light.
CRACK!
What was that?
It's okay, Spark. It's just a little thunder and lightning from a passing storm.
WHIMPER... WHIMPERRR...
Actually, Spark, if you could understand how light works, things like lightning wouldn't be so scary.

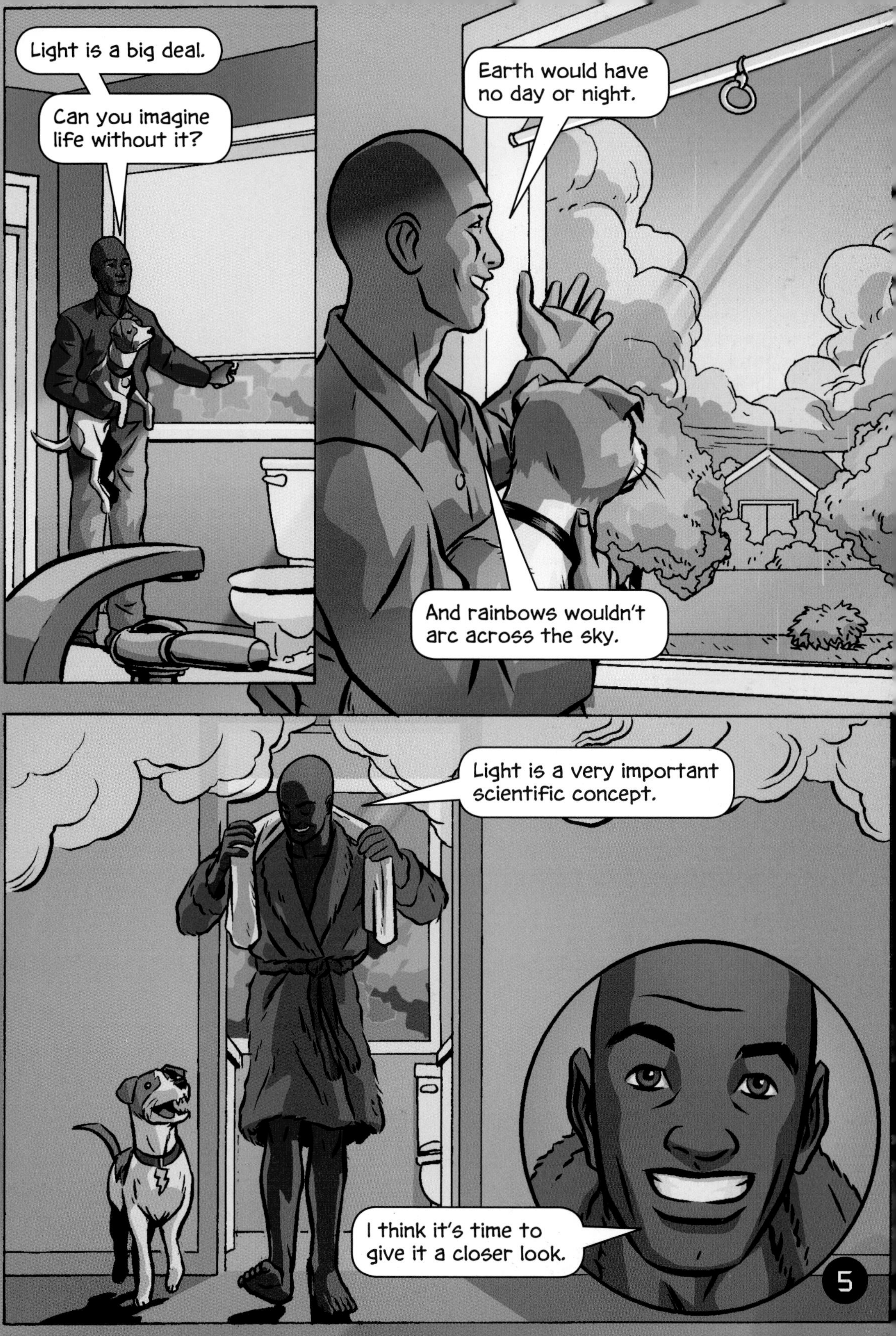
Light is a big deal.
Can you imagine life without it?
Earth would have no day or night.
And rainbows wouldn't arc across the sky.
Light is a very important scientific concept.
I think it's time to give it a closer look.

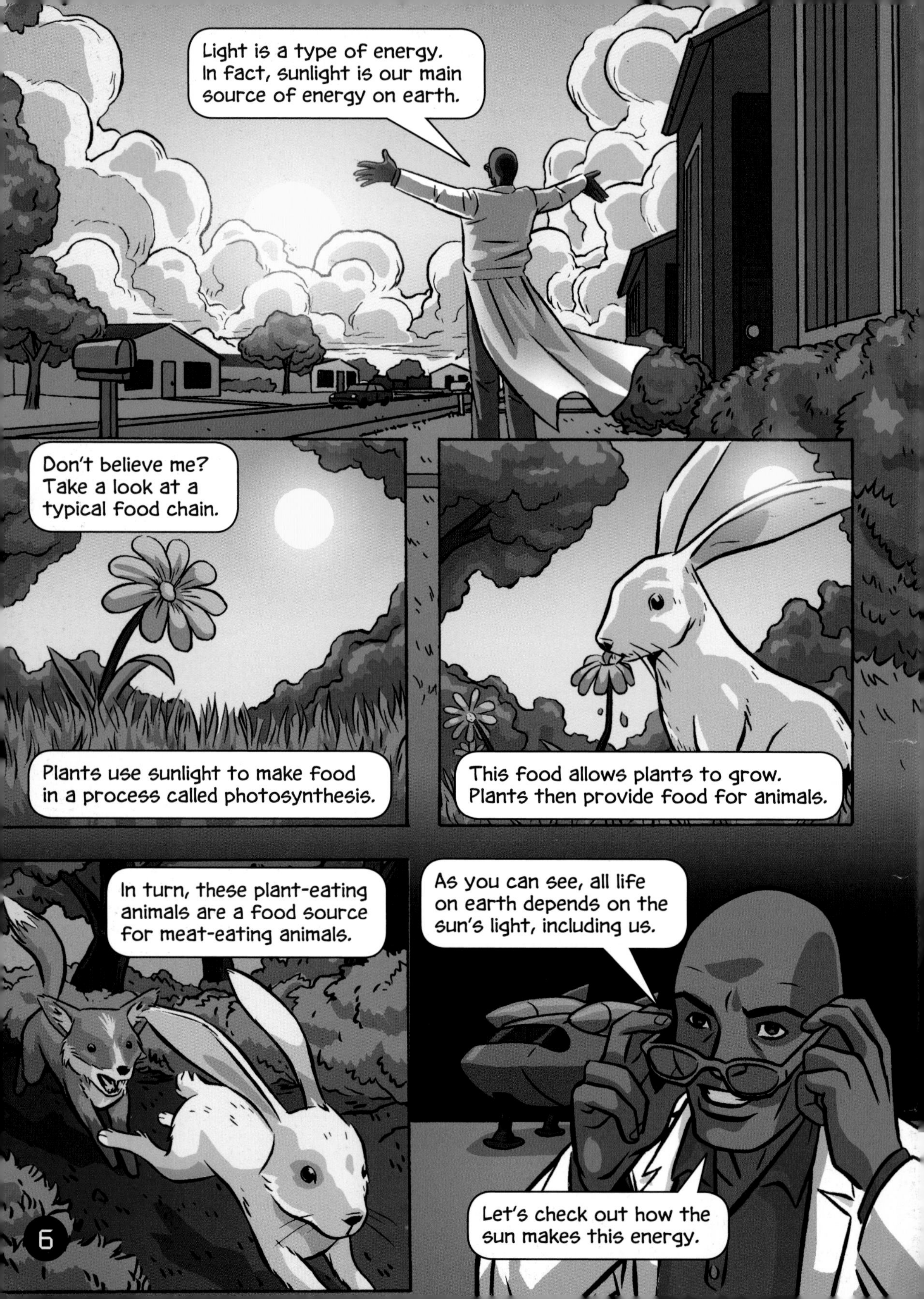
Light is a type of energy. In fact, sunlight is our main source of energy on earth.
Don't believe me? Take a look at a typical food chain.
Plants use sunlight to make food in a process called photosynthesis.
This food allows plants to grow. Plants then provide food for animals.
In turn, these plant-eating animals are a food source for meat-eating animals.
As you can see, all life on earth depends on the sun's light, including us.
Let's check out how the sun makes this energy.

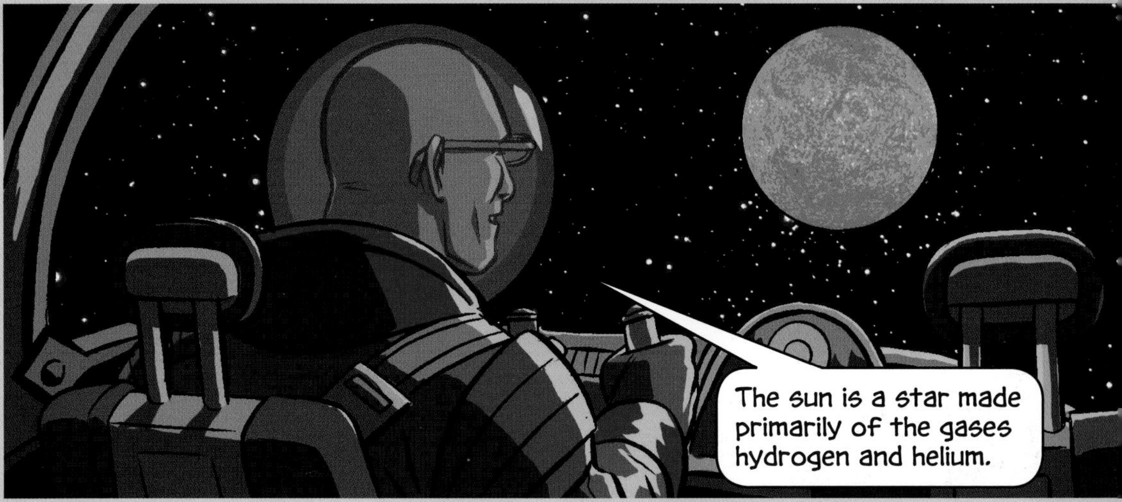
The sun is a star made primarily of the gases hydrogen and helium.

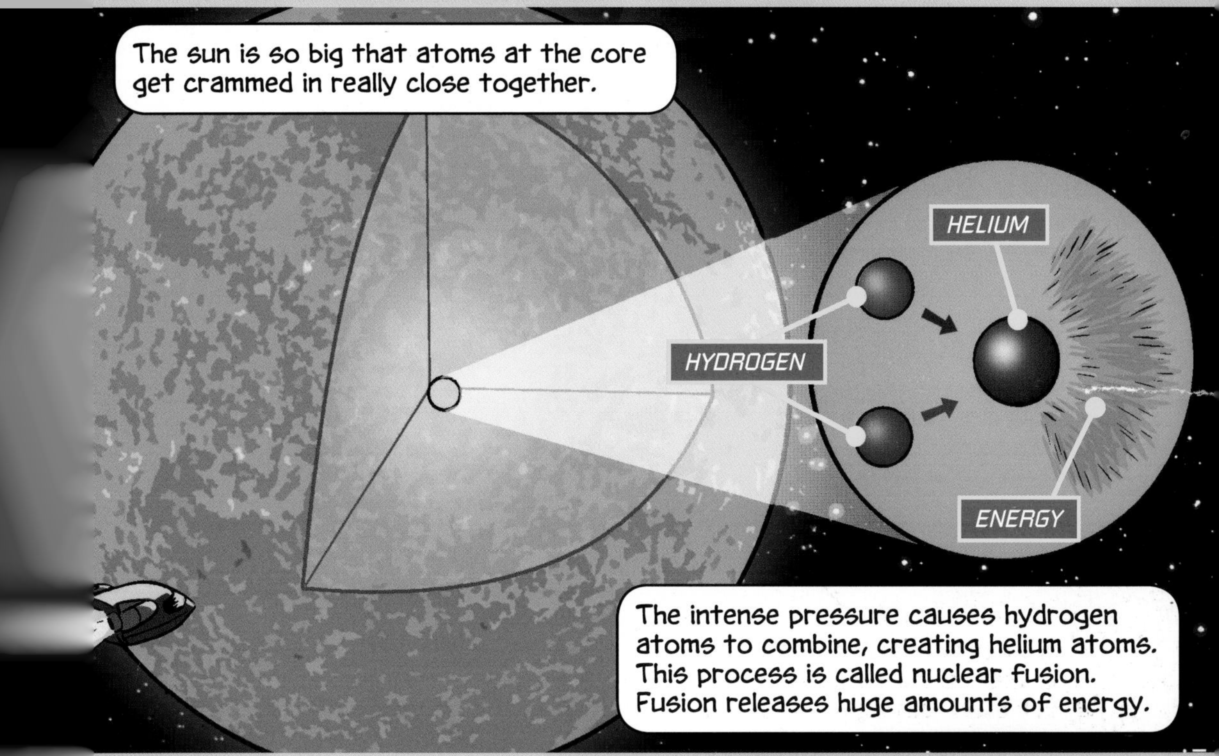
The sun is so big that atoms at the core get crammed in really close together.
HELIUM
HYDROGEN
ENERGY
The intense pressure causes hydrogen atoms to combine, creating helium atoms. This process is called nuclear fusion. Fusion releases huge amounts of energy.

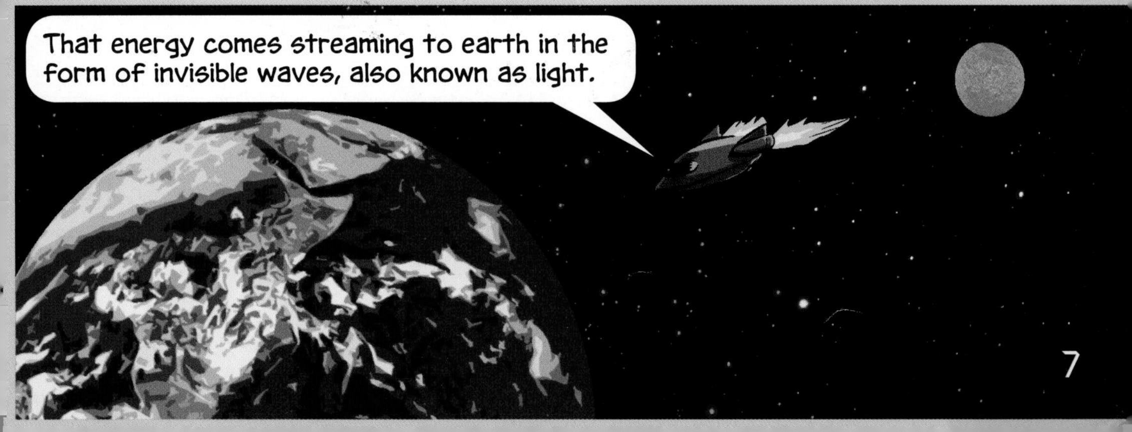
That energy comes streaming to earth in the form of invisible waves, also known as light.

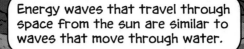

Energy waves that travel through space from the sun are similar to waves that move through water.

We call the length of a wave its wavelength.

We measure wavelengths by the distance between two wave peaks.

WAVELENGTH

WAVELENGTH

Smaller wavelengths move more quickly and carry more energy than larger ones.

Sunlight includes wavelengths that are very small, very large, and everything in between.

Like water waves, light waves with short wavelengths have more energy than waves with long wavelengths.

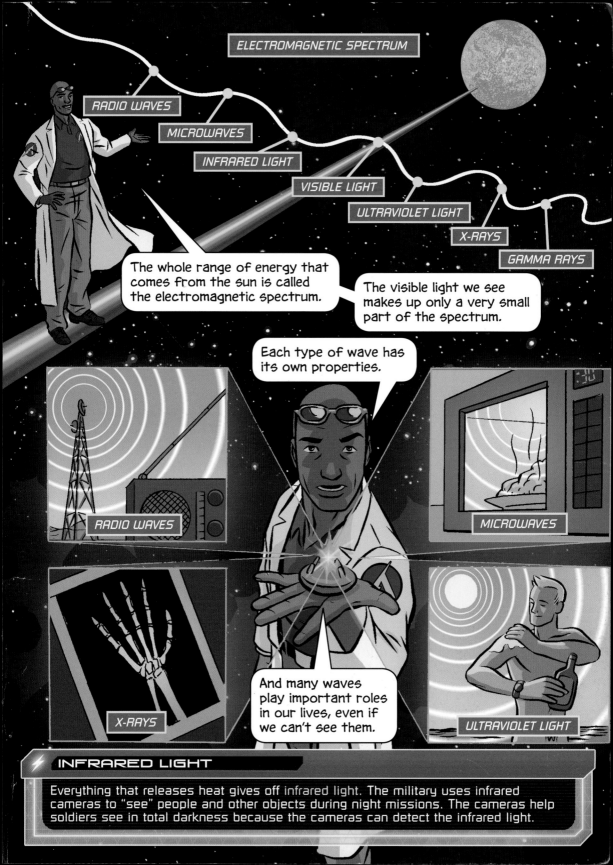

ELECTROMAGNETIC SPECTRUM

RADIO WAVES

MICROWAVES

INFRARED LIGHT

VISIBLE LIGHT

ULTRAVIOLET LIGHT

X-RAYS

GAMMA RAYS

The whole range of energy that comes from the sun is called the electromagnetic spectrum.

The visible light we see makes up only a very small part of the spectrum.

Each type of wave has its own properties.

RADIO WAVES

MICROWAVES

X-RAYS

And many waves play important roles in our lives, even if we can't see them.

ULTRAVIOLET LIGHT

INFRARED LIGHT

Everything that releases heat gives off infrared light. The military uses infrared cameras to "see" people and other objects during night missions. The cameras help soldiers see in total darkness because the cameras can detect the infrared light.

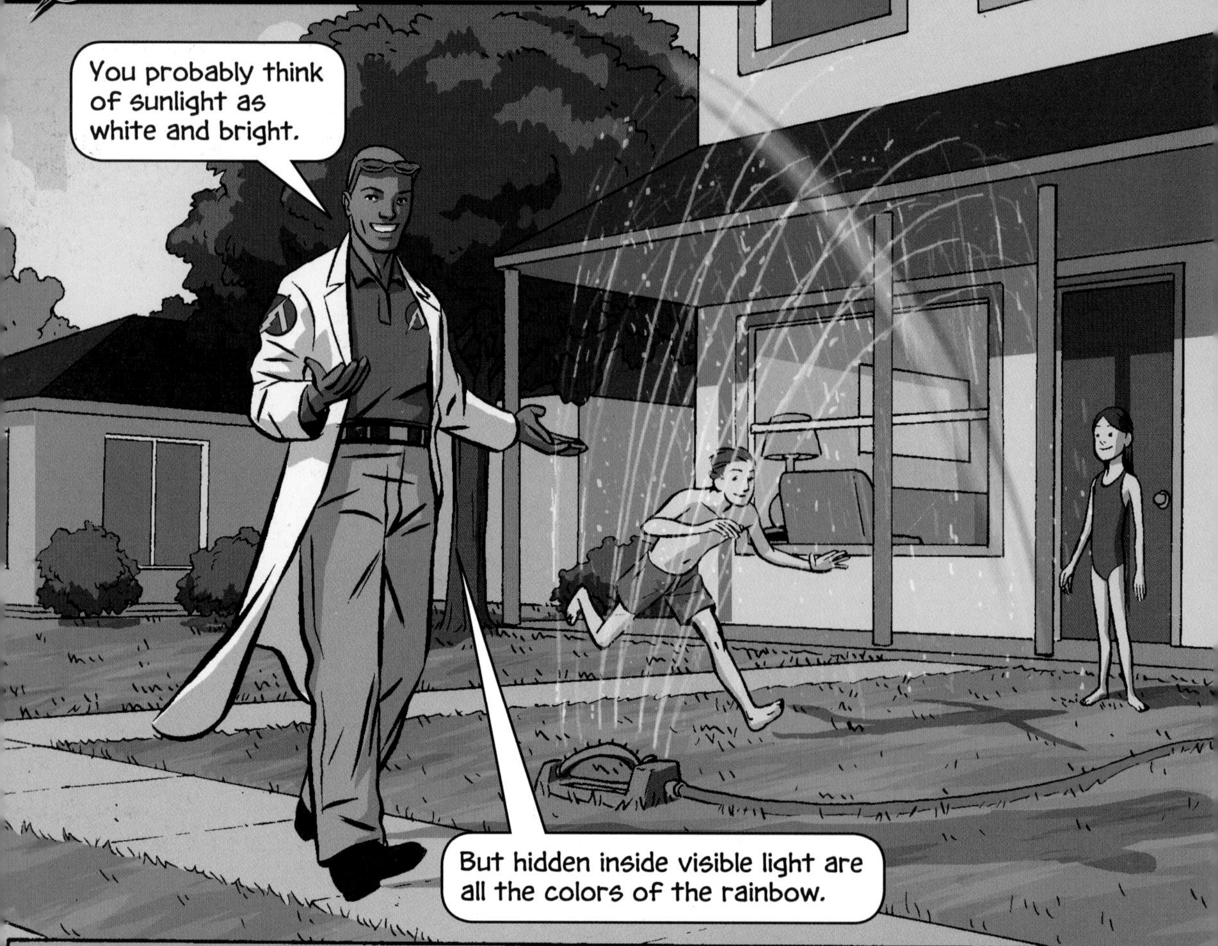
You probably think of sunlight as white and bright.
But hidden inside visible light are all the colors of the rainbow.

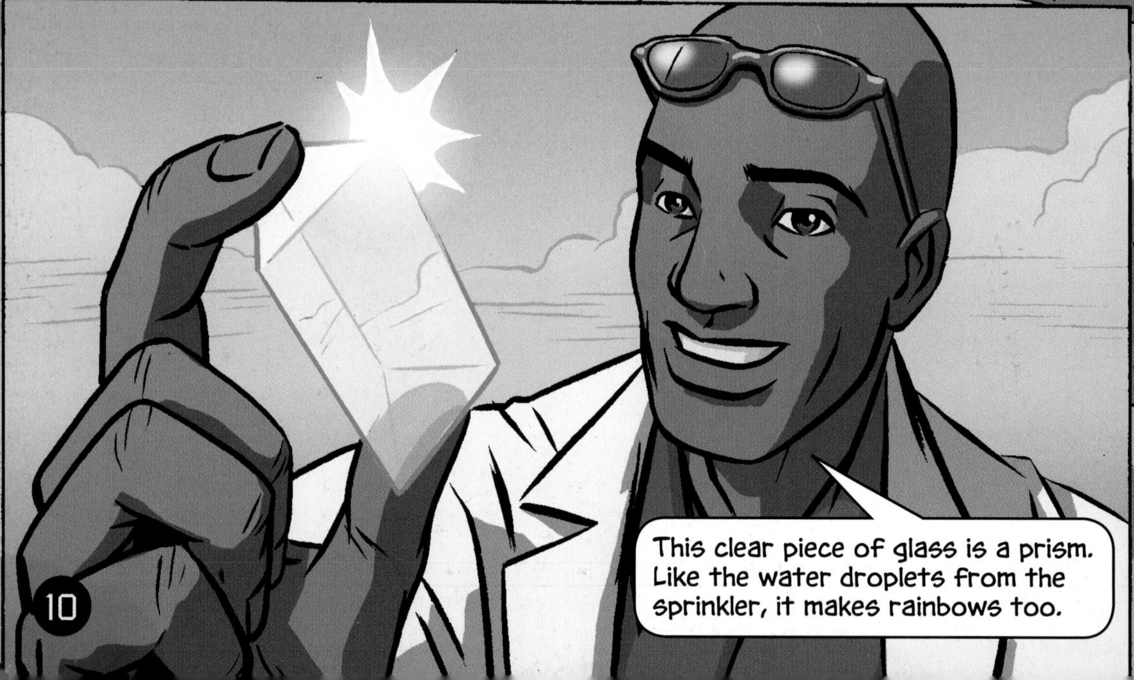
This clear piece of glass is a prism. Like the water droplets from the sprinkler, it makes rainbows too.

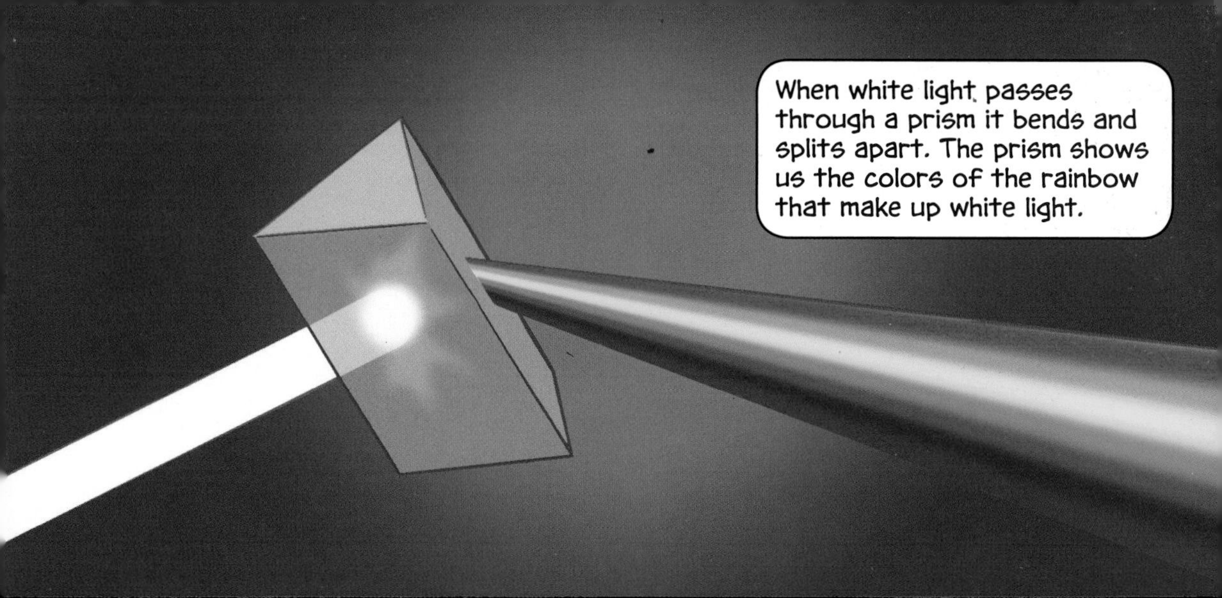
When white light passes through a prism it bends and splits apart. The prism shows us the colors of the rainbow that make up white light.

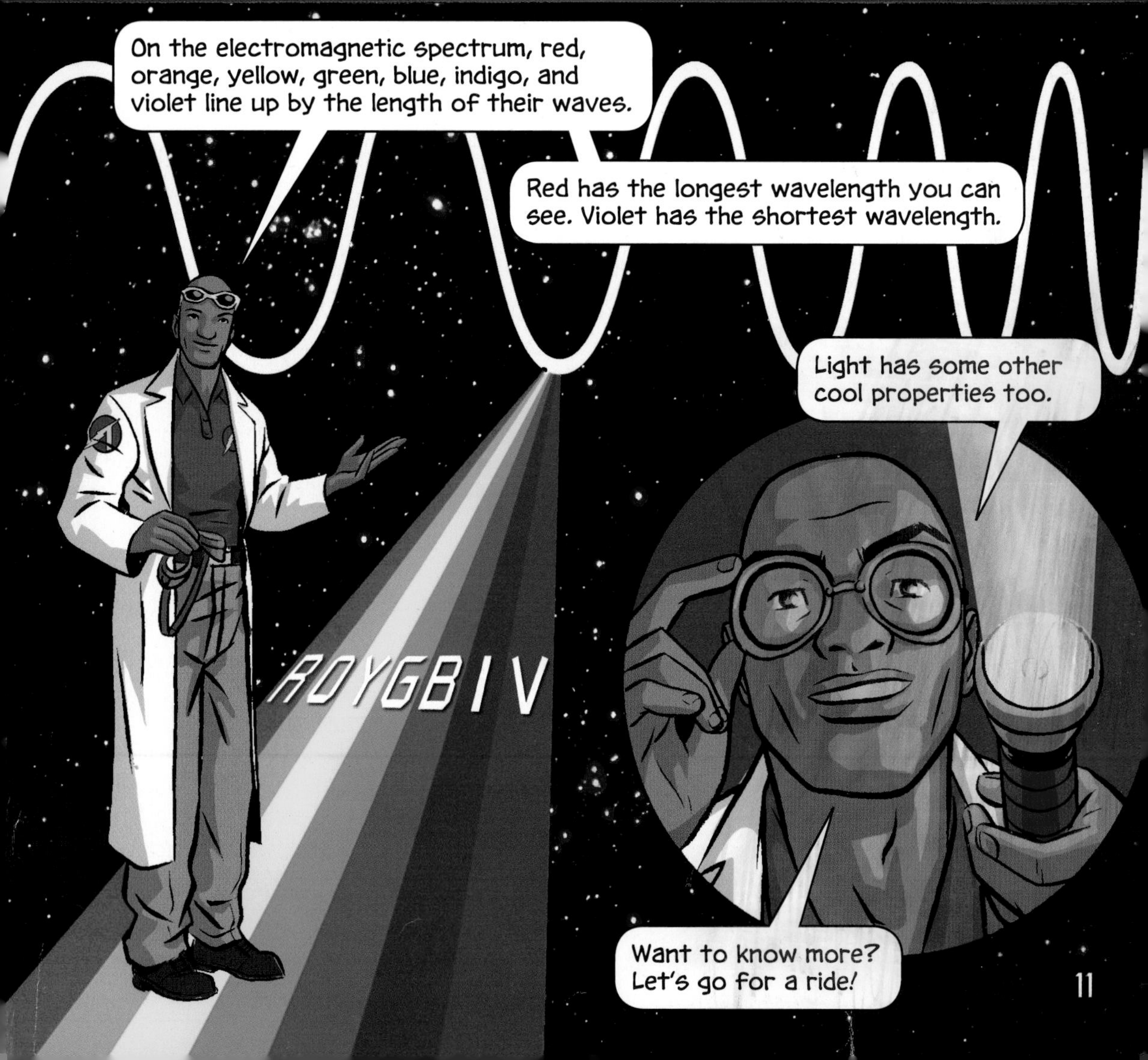
On the electromagnetic spectrum, red, orange, yellow, green, blue, indigo, and violet line up by the length of their waves.
Red has the longest wavelength you can see. Violet has the shortest wavelength.
ROYGBIV
Light has some other cool properties too.
Want to know more? Let's go for a ride!

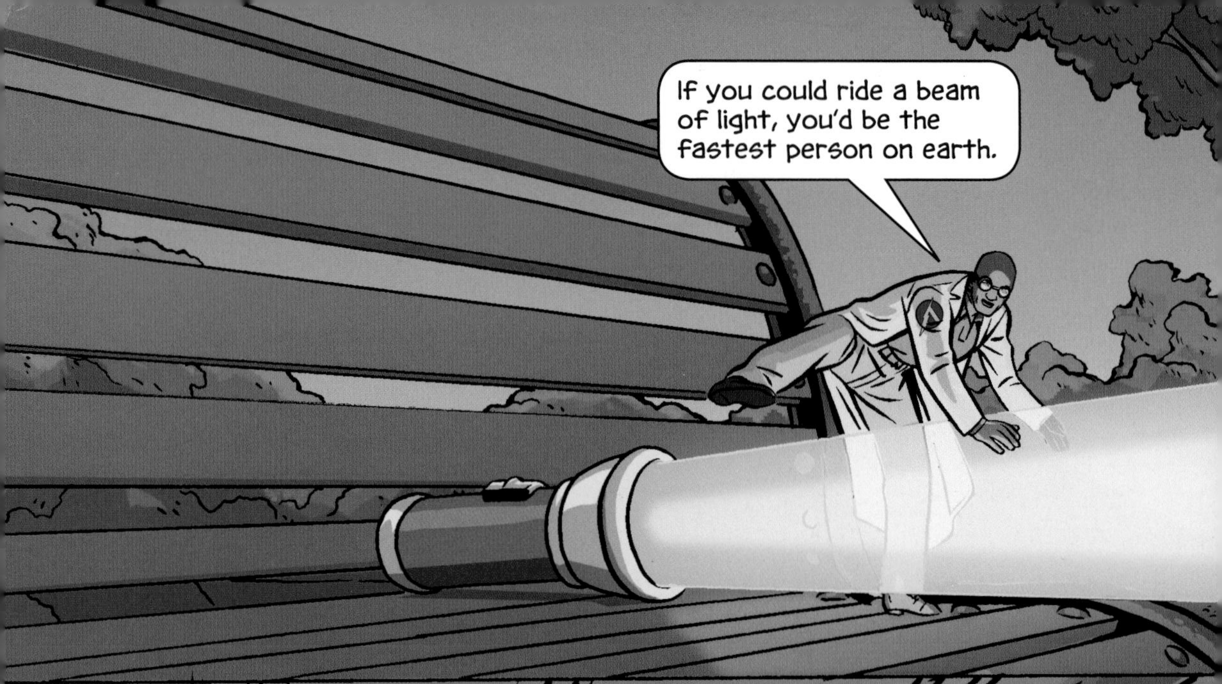
If you could ride a beam of light, you'd be the fastest person on earth.

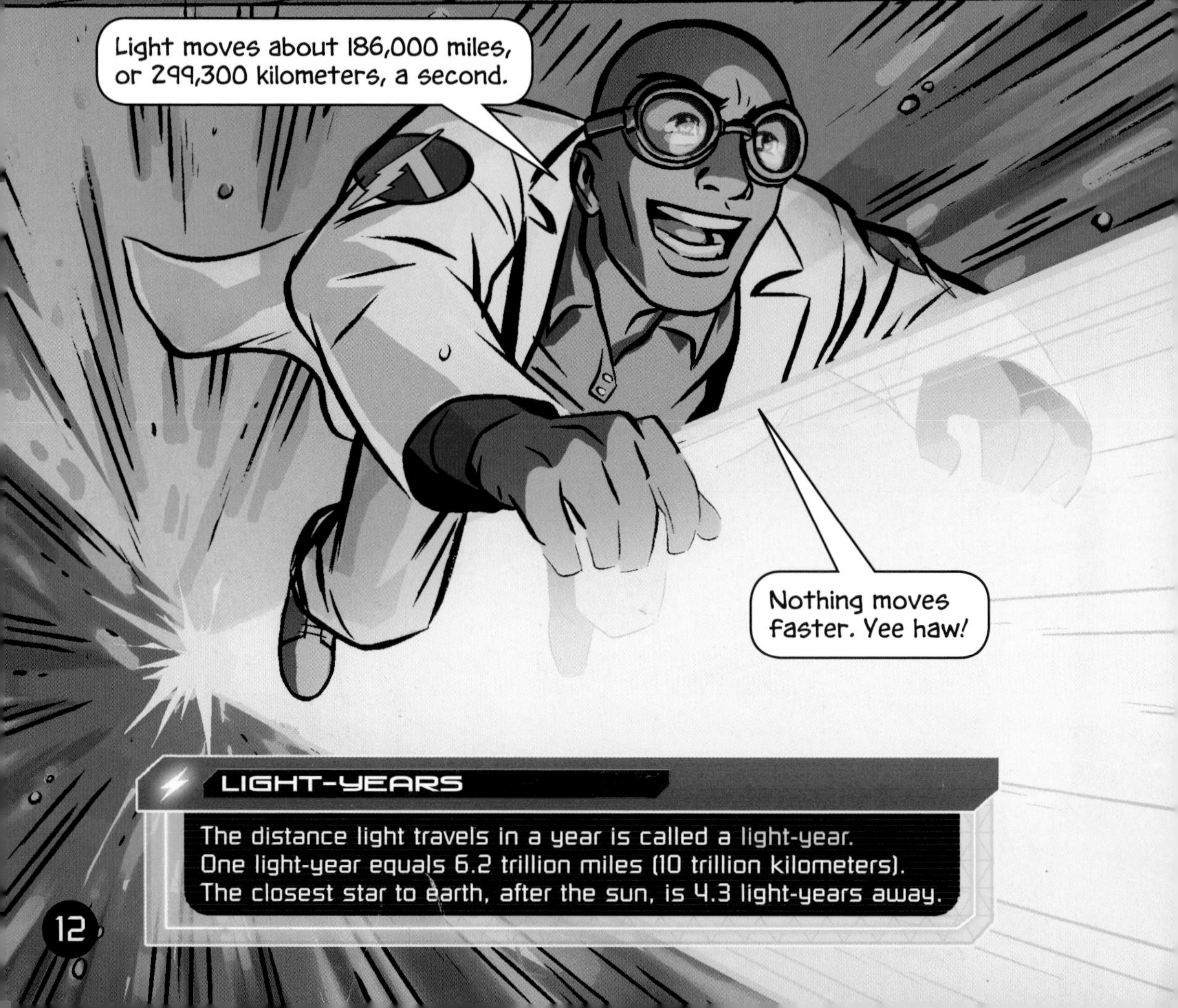
Light moves about 186,000 miles, or 299,300 kilometers, a second.
Nothing moves faster. Yee haw!

LIGHT-YEARS

The distance light travels in a year is called a light-year. One light-year equals 6.2 trillion miles (10 trillion kilometers). The closest star to earth, after the sun, is 4.3 light-years away.

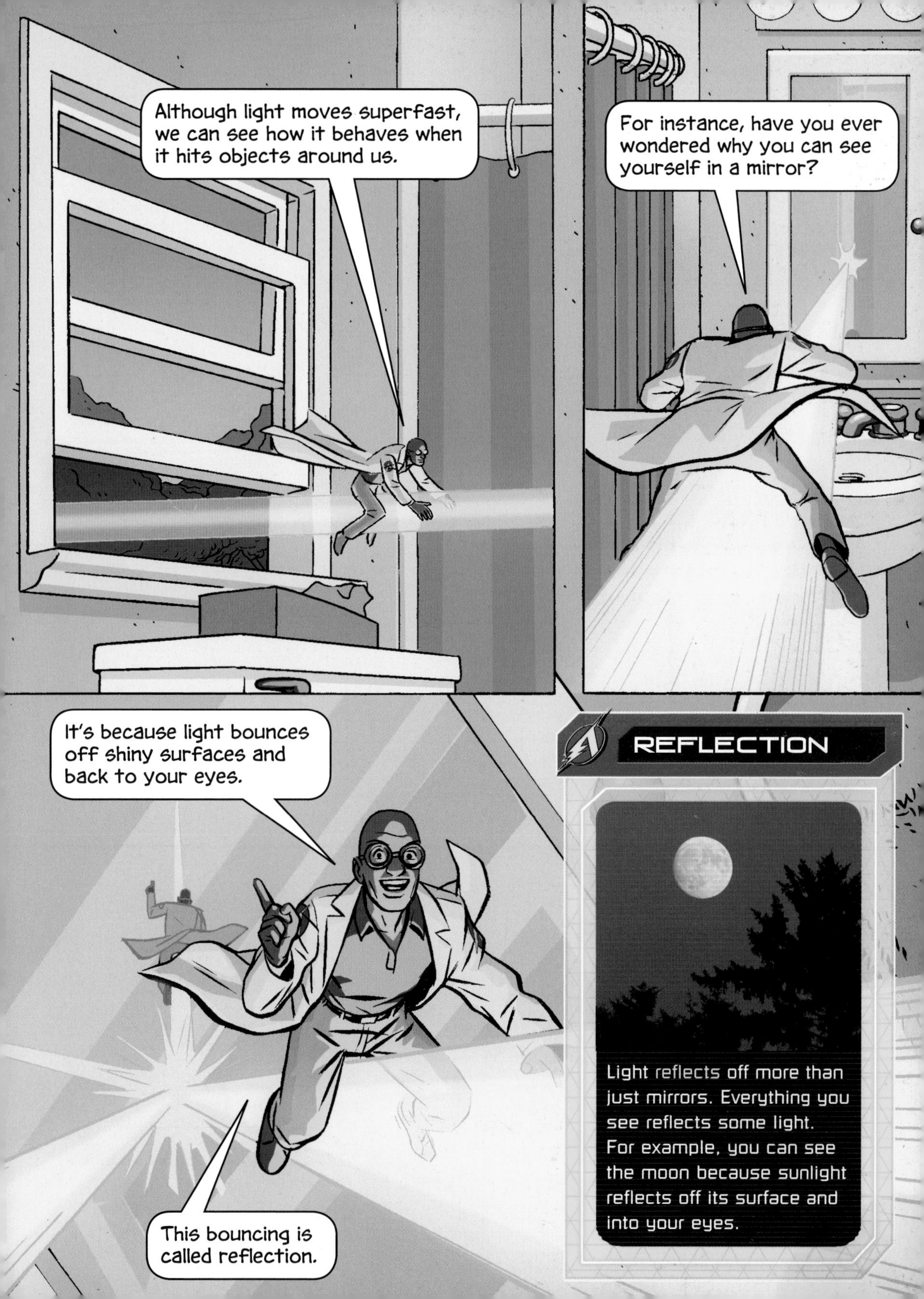
Although light moves superfast, we can see how it behaves when it hits objects around us.
For instance, have you ever wondered why you can see yourself in a mirror?
It's because light bounces off shiny surfaces and back to your eyes.
This bouncing is called reflection.
REFLECTION
Light reflects off more than just mirrors. Everything you see reflects some light. For example, you can see the moon because sunlight reflects off its surface and into your eyes.

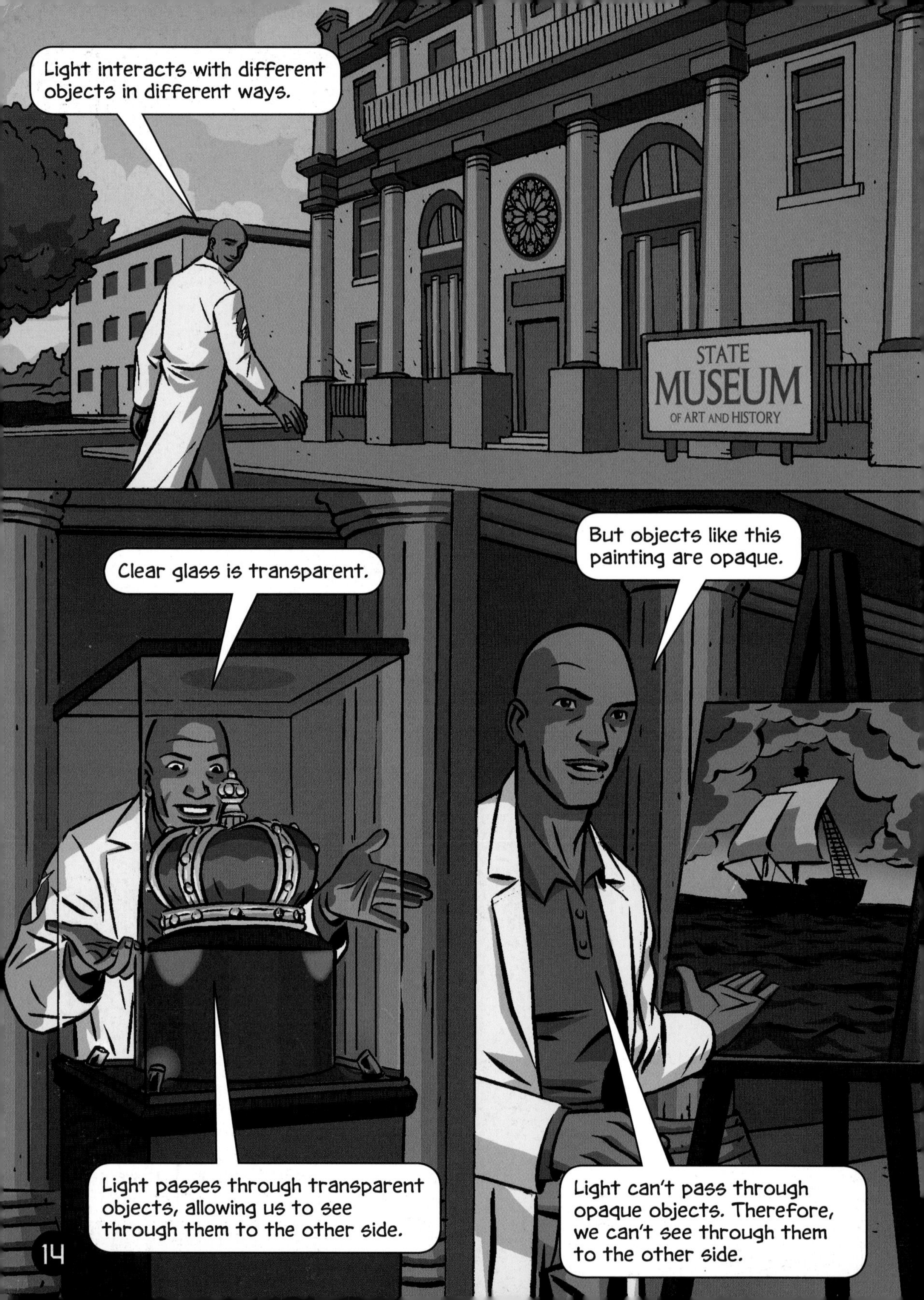
Light interacts with different objects in different ways.
STATE MUSEUM OF ART AND HISTORY
Clear glass is transparent.
Light passes through transparent objects, allowing us to see through them to the other side.
But objects like this painting are opaque.
Light can't pass through opaque objects. Therefore, we can't see through them to the other side.

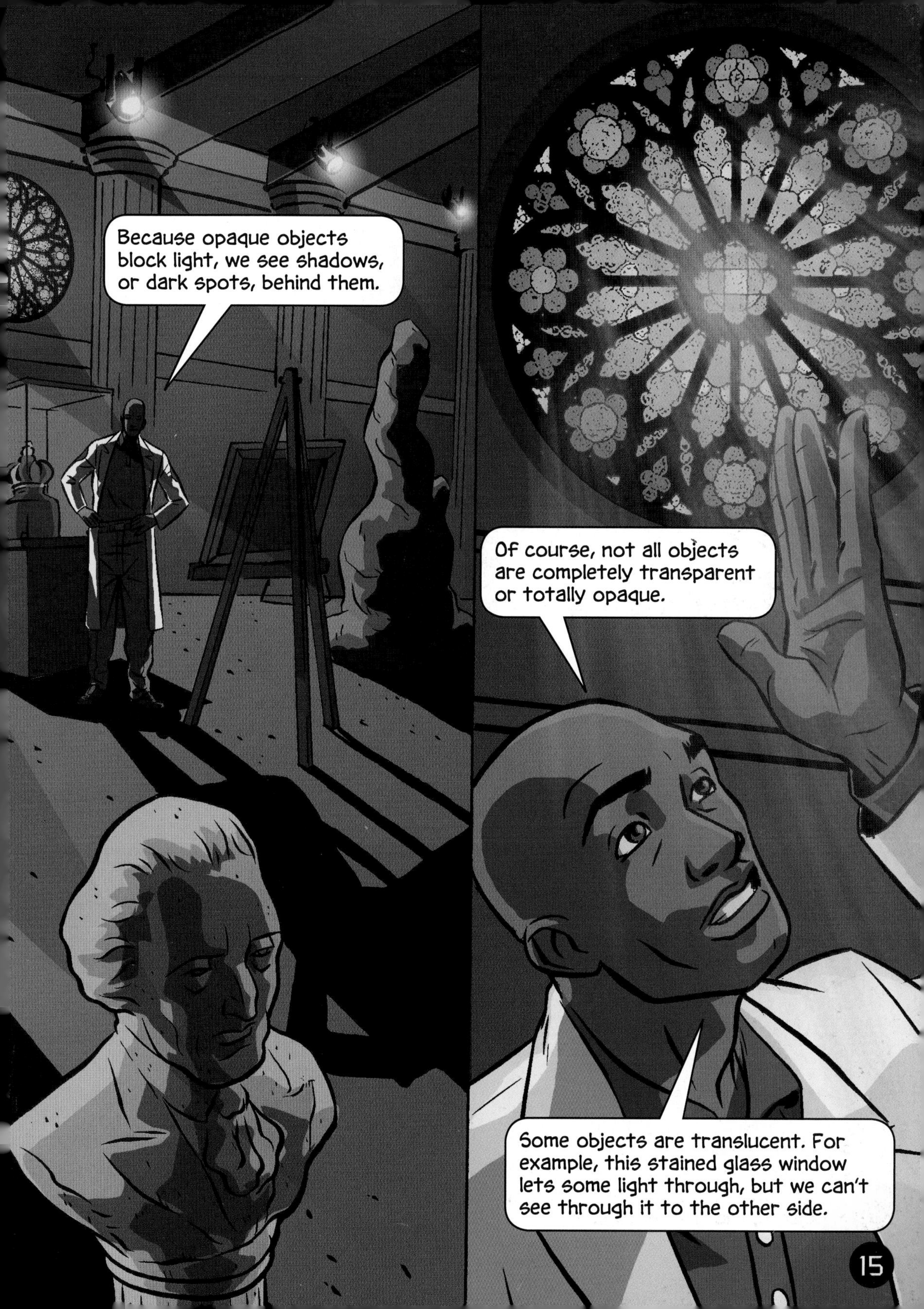
Because opaque objects block light, we see shadows, or dark spots, behind them.
Of course, not all objects are completely transparent or totally opaque.
Some objects are translucent. For example, this stained glass window lets some light through, but we can't see through it to the other side.

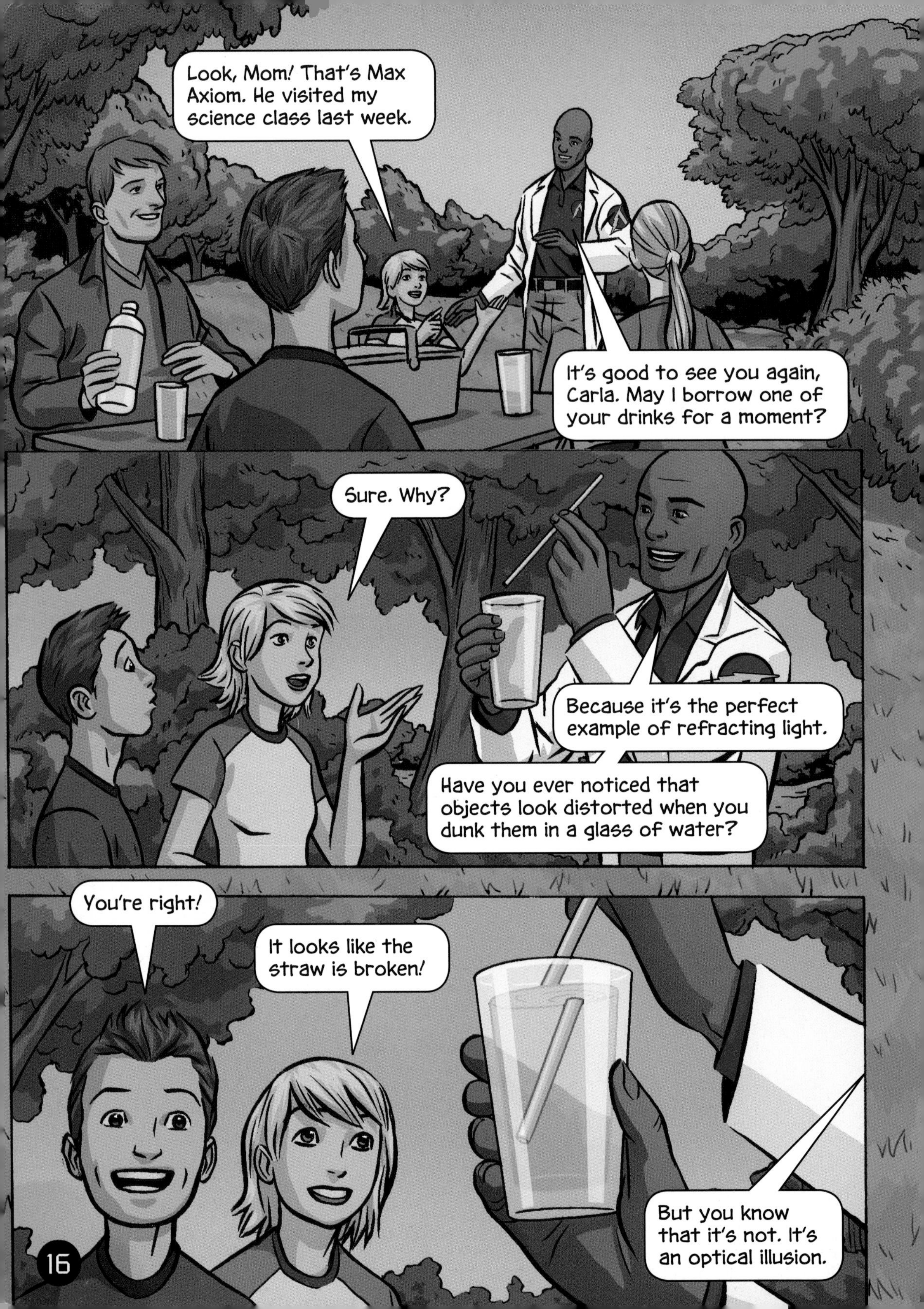

Look, Mom! That's Max Axiom. He visited my science class last week.
It's good to see you again, Carla. May I borrow one of your drinks for a moment?
Sure. Why?
Because it's the perfect example of refracting light.
Have you ever noticed that objects look distorted when you dunk them in a glass of water?
You're right!
It looks like the straw is broken!
But you know that it's not. It's an optical illusion.

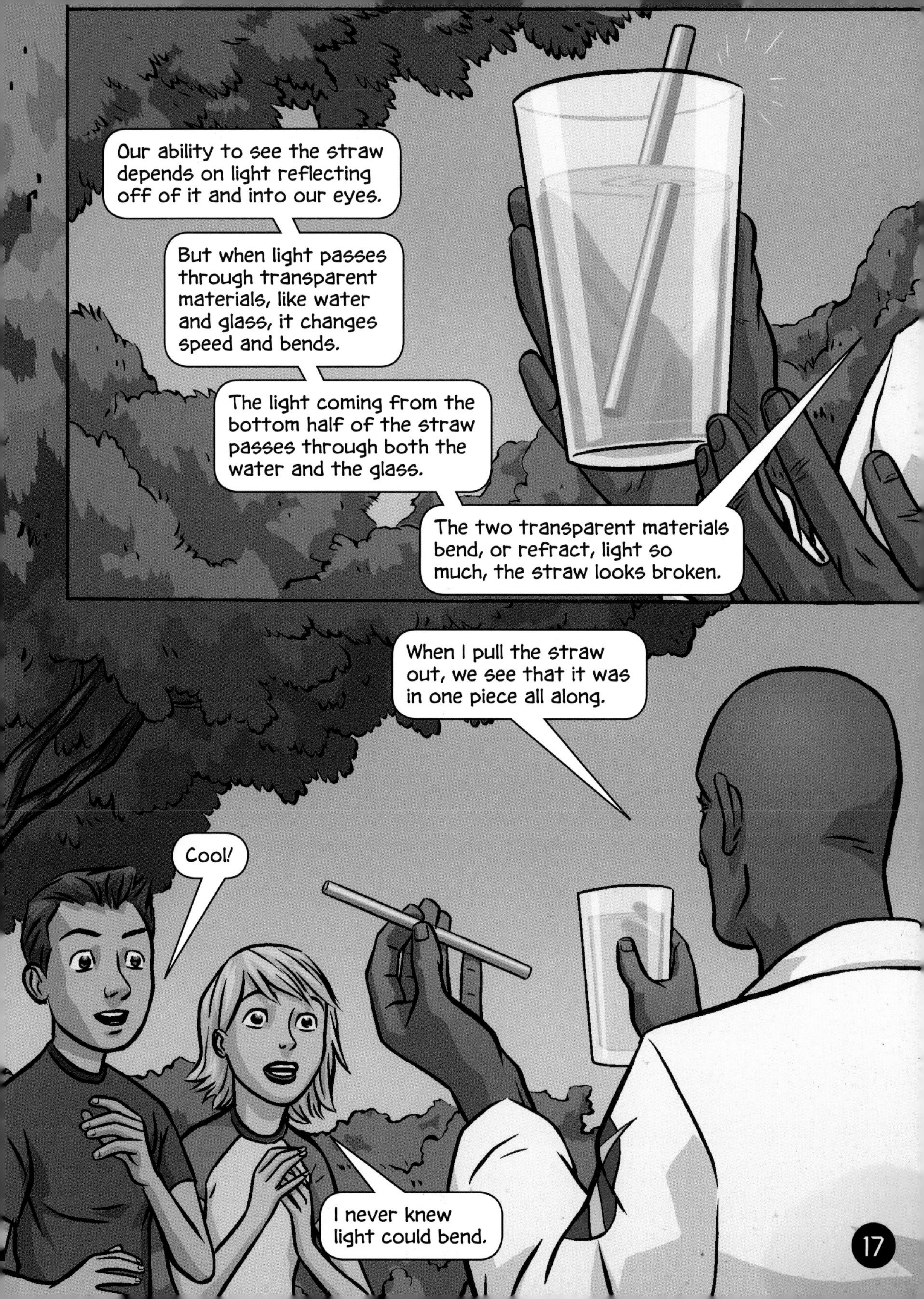
Our ability to see the straw depends on light reflecting off of it and into our eyes.
But when light passes through transparent materials, like water and glass, it changes speed and bends.
The light coming from the bottom half of the straw passes through both the water and the glass.
The two transparent materials bend, or refract, light so much, the straw looks broken.
When I pull the straw out, we see that it was in one piece all along.
Cool!
I never knew light could bend.

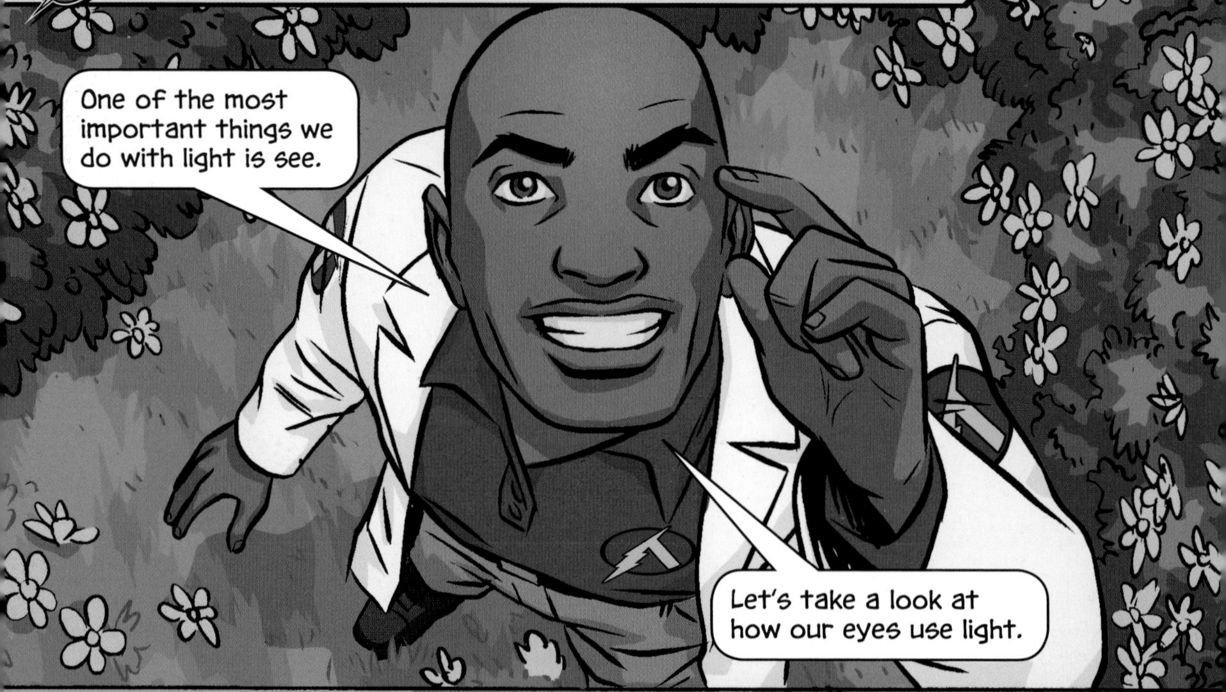
One of the most important things we do with light is see.
Let's take a look at how our eyes use light.

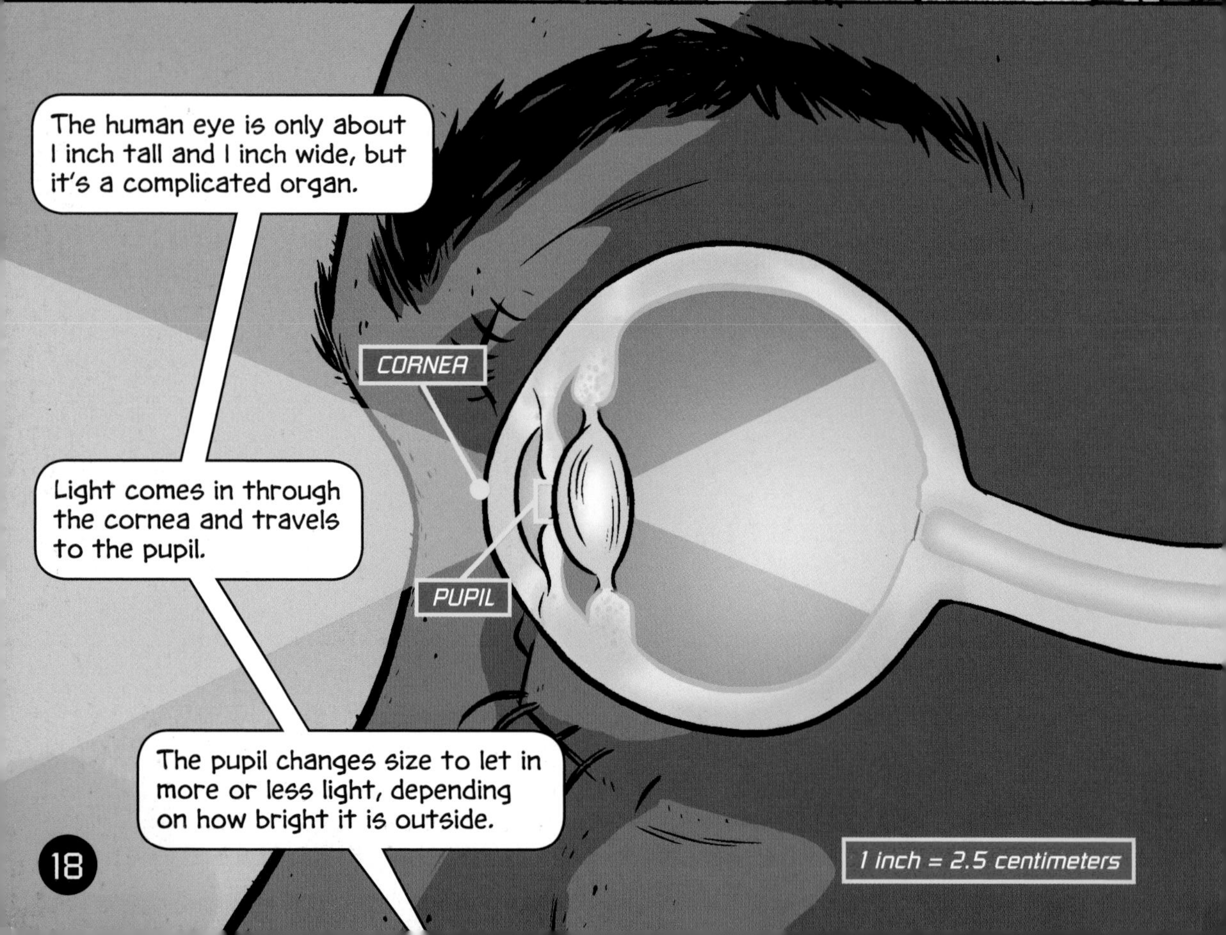
The human eye is only about 1 inch tall and 1 inch wide, but it's a complicated organ.
CORNEA
Light comes in through the cornea and travels to the pupil.
PUPIL
The pupil changes size to let in more or less light, depending on how bright it is outside.
1 inch = 2.5 centimeters

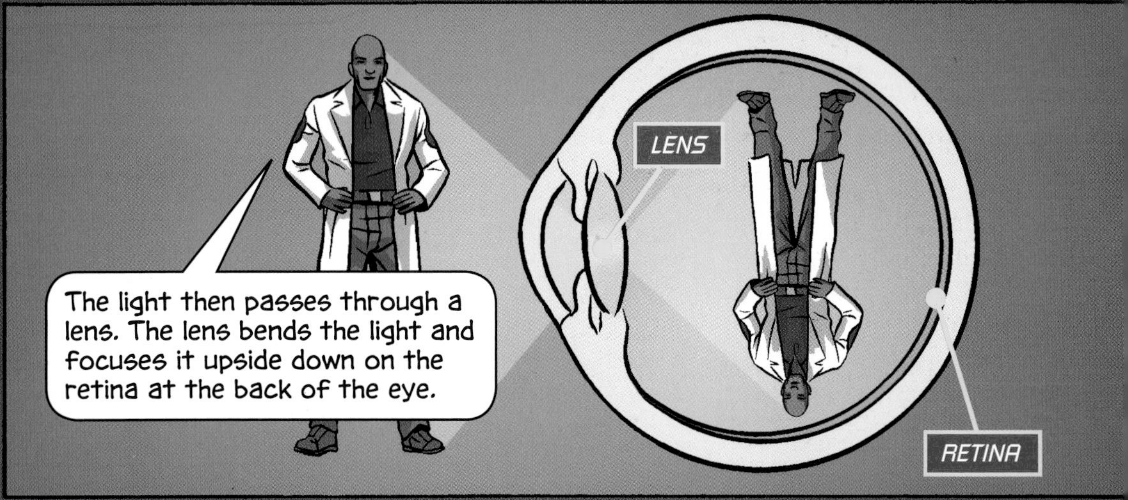
The light then passes through a lens. The lens bends the light and focuses it upside down on the retina at the back of the eye.
LENS
RETINA

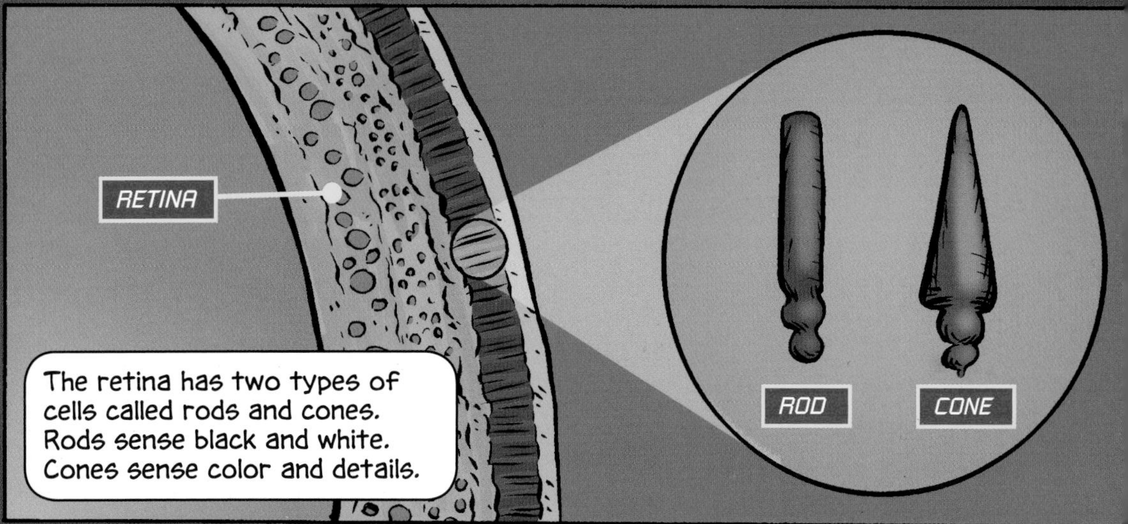
RETINA
ROD
CONE
The retina has two types of cells called rods and cones. Rods sense black and white. Cones sense color and details.

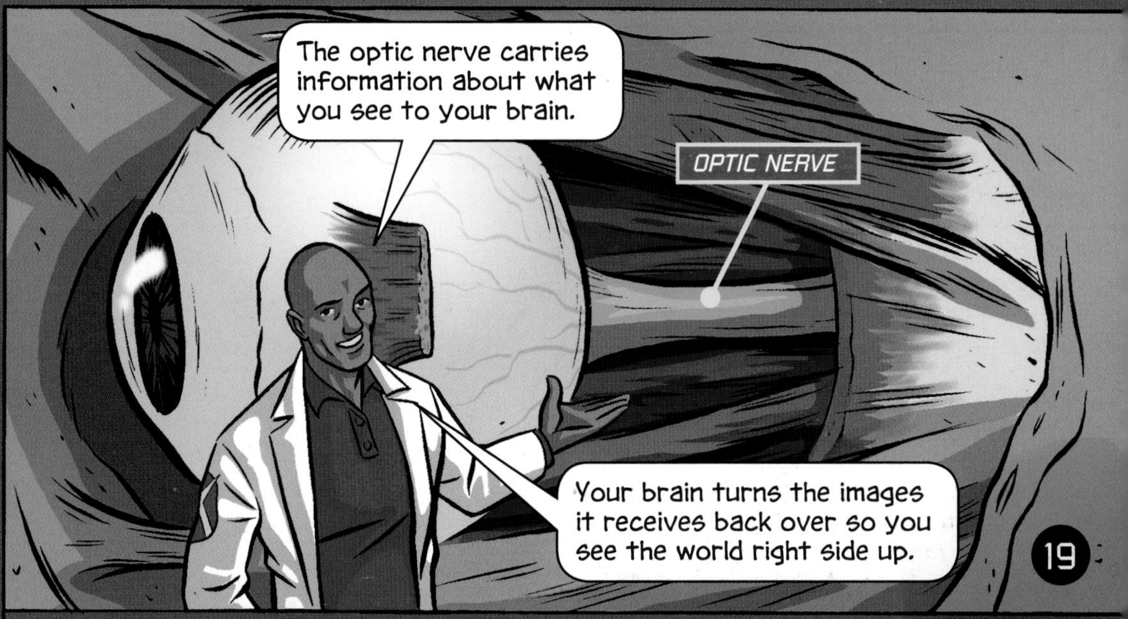
The optic nerve carries information about what you see to your brain.
OPTIC NERVE
Your brain turns the images it receives back over so you see the world right side up.

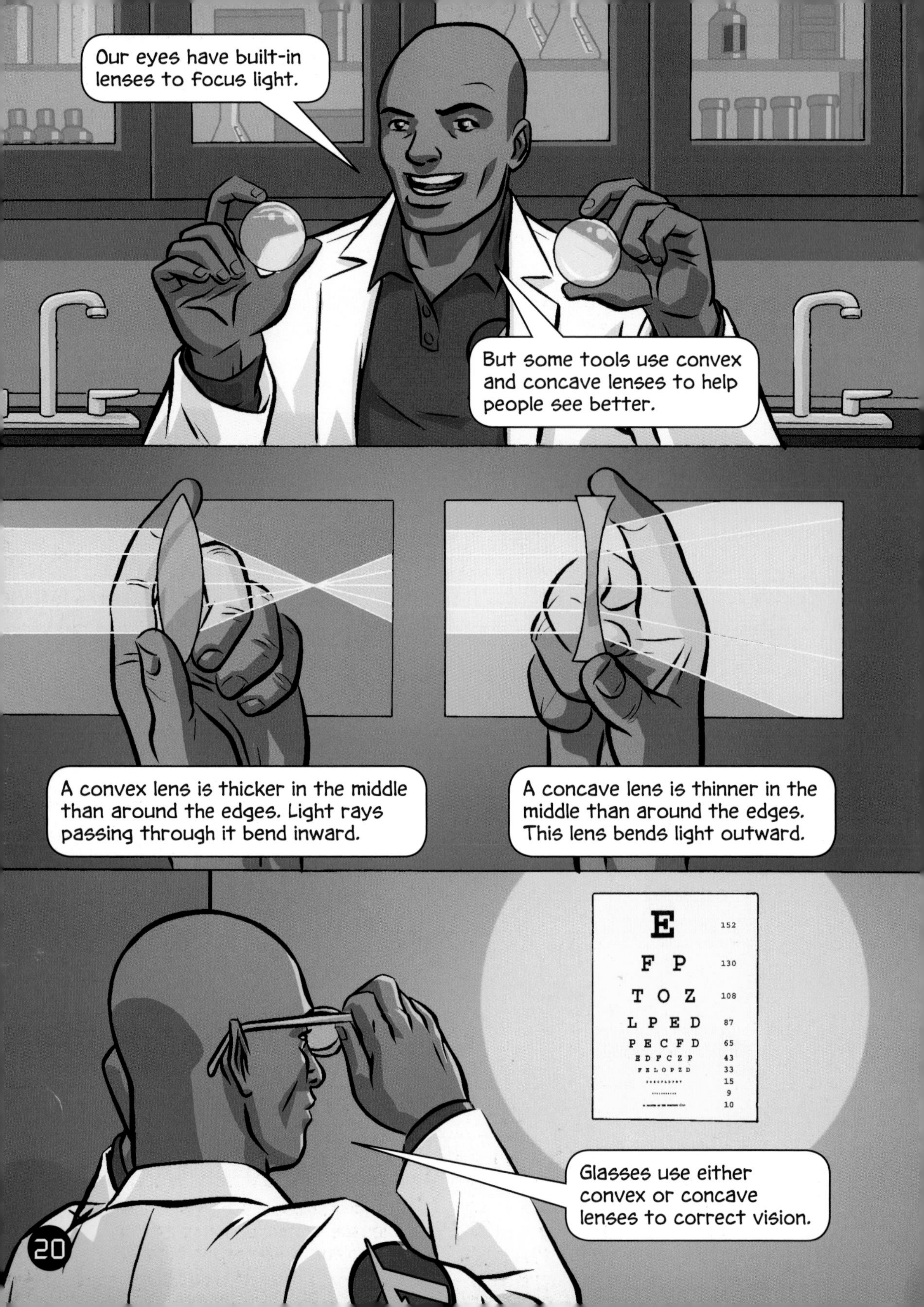
Our eyes have built-in lenses to focus light.
But some tools use convex and concave lenses to help people see better.
A convex lens is thicker in the middle than around the edges. Light rays passing through it bend inward.
A concave lens is thinner in the middle than around the edges. This lens bends light outward.
E 152
F P 130
T O Z 108
L P E D 87
P E C F D 65
E D F C Z P 43
F E L O P Z D 33
15
9
10
Glasses use either convex or concave lenses to correct vision.

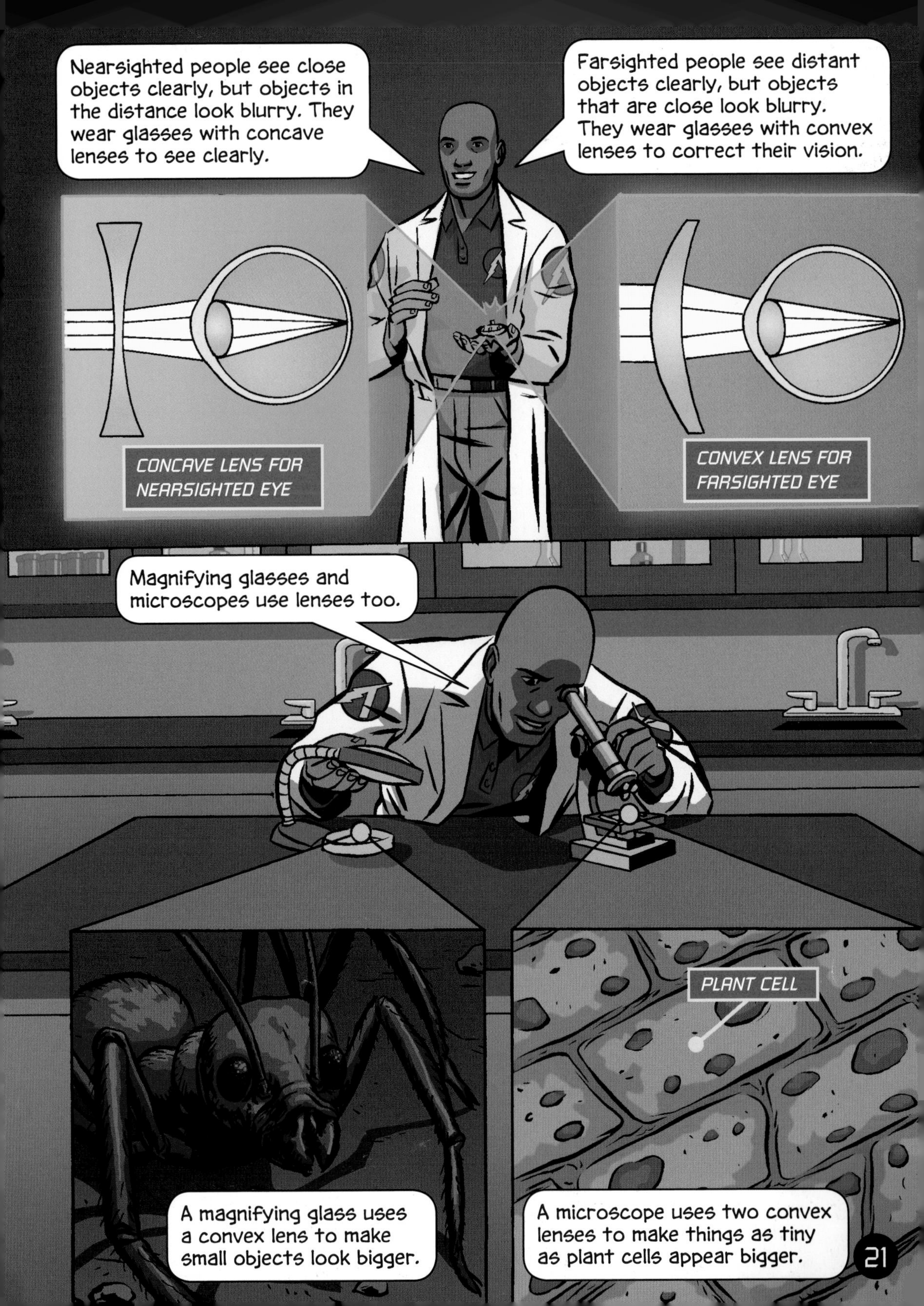
Nearsighted people see close objects clearly, but objects in the distance look blurry. They wear glasses with concave lenses to see clearly.
Farsighted people see distant objects clearly, but objects that are close look blurry. They wear glasses with convex lenses to correct their vision.
CONCAVE LENS FOR NEARSIGHTED EYE
CONVEX LENS FOR FARSIGHTED EYE
Magnifying glasses and microscopes use lenses too.
PLANT CELL
A magnifying glass uses a convex lens to make small objects look bigger.
A microscope uses two convex lenses to make things as tiny as plant cells appear bigger.

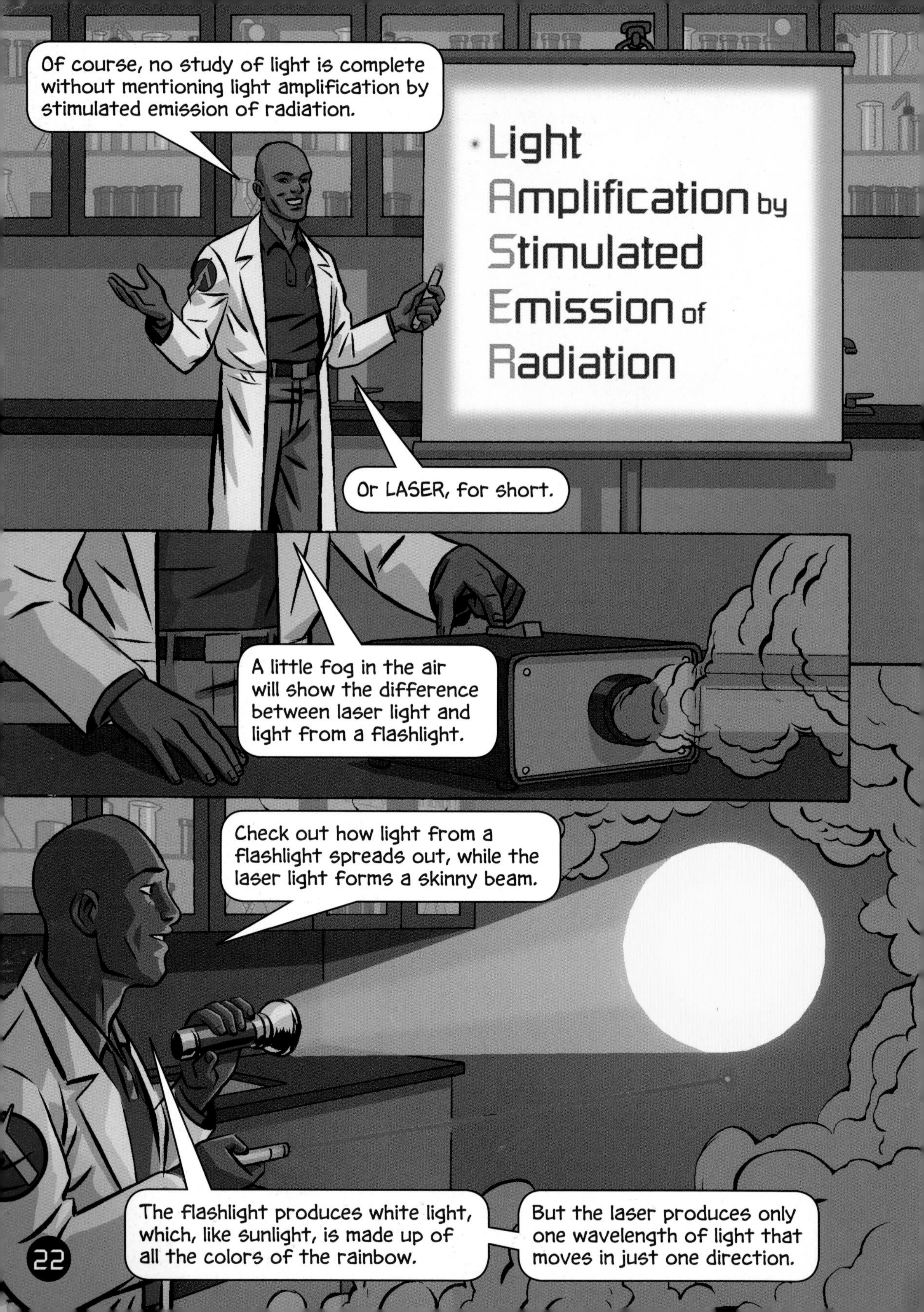
Of course, no study of light is complete without mentioning light amplification by stimulated emission of radiation.
Light Amplification by Stimulated Emission of Radiation
Or LASER, for short.
A little fog in the air will show the difference between laser light and light from a flashlight.
Check out how light from a flashlight spreads out, while the laser light forms a skinny beam.
The flashlight produces white light, which, like sunlight, is made up of all the colors of the rainbow.
But the laser produces only one wavelength of light that moves in just one direction.

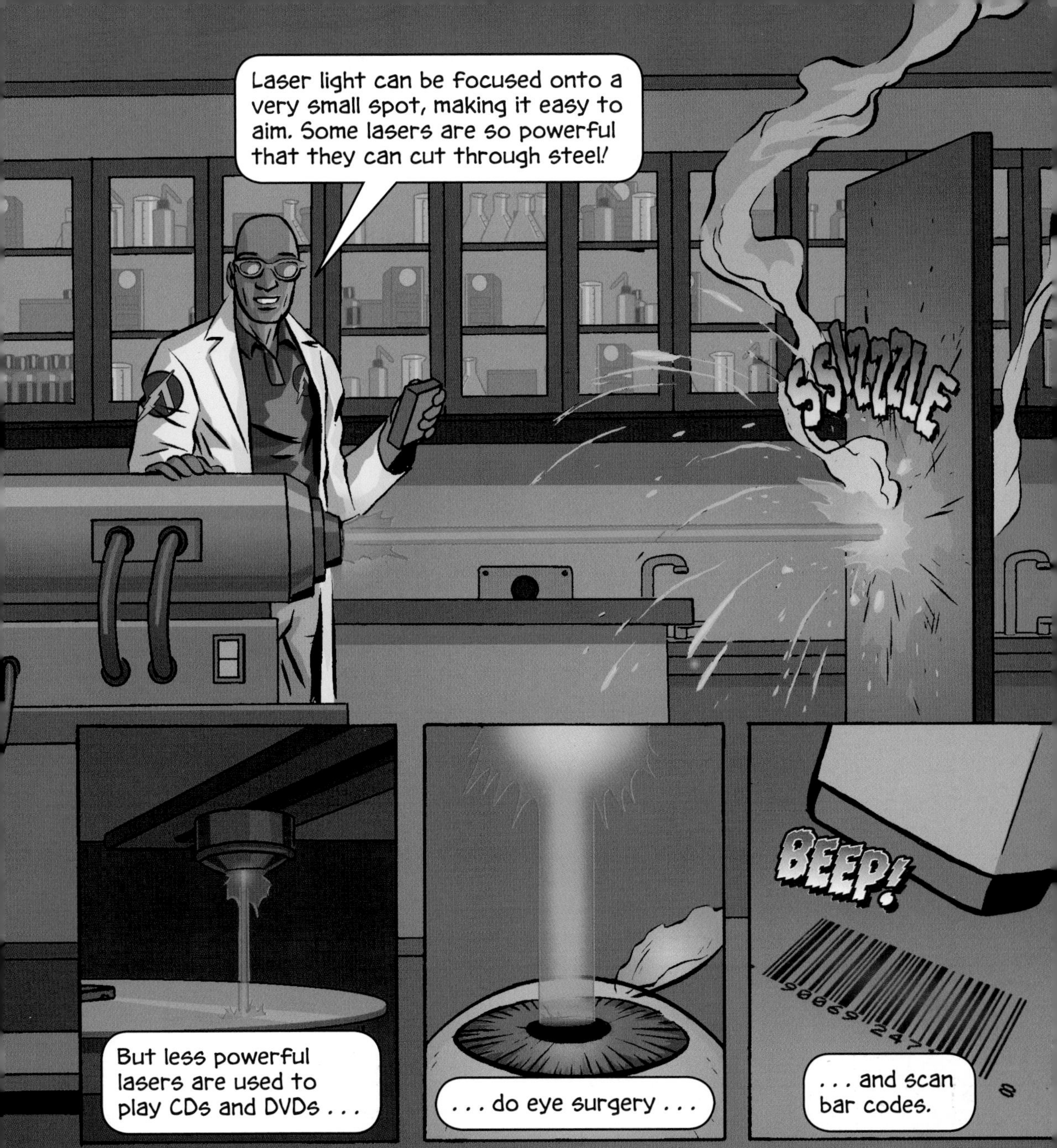
Laser light can be focused onto a very small spot, making it easy to aim. Some lasers are so powerful that they can cut through steel!
SSIZZZLE
But less powerful lasers are used to play CDs and DVDs . . .
. . . do eye surgery . . .
BEEP!
. . . and scan bar codes.

MORE ABOUT LASERS

ACCESS GRANTED: MAX AXIOM

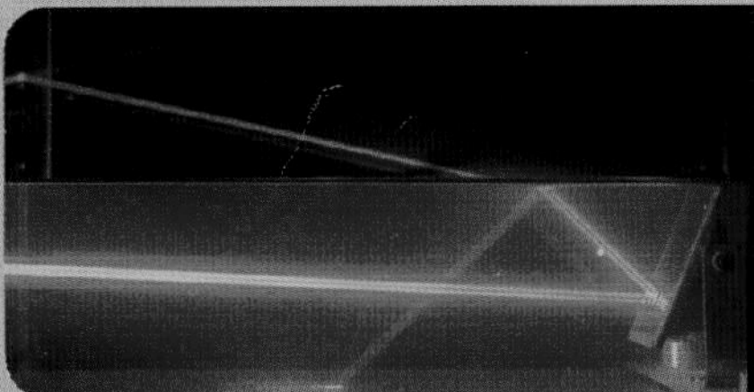

Lasers use mirrors to bounce light back and forth until it is all moving in one focused direction. The types of atoms inside a laser determine what wavelength will come out. Ruby-filled lasers give off red light. Carbon dioxide-filled lasers give off infrared light, which can be hot enough to cut metal.

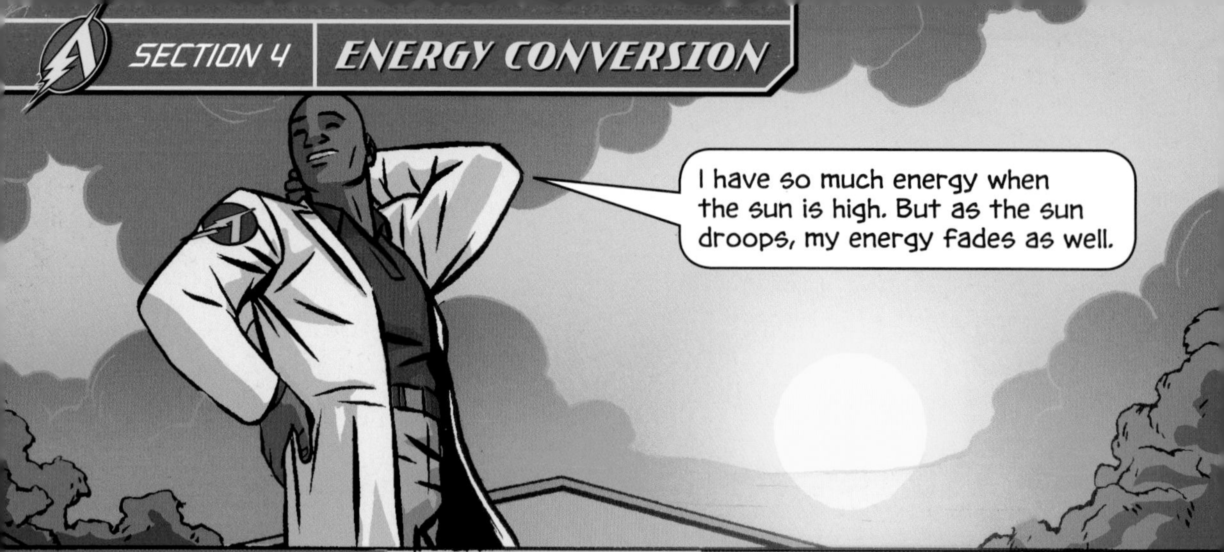
I have so much energy when the sun is high. But as the sun droops, my energy fades as well.

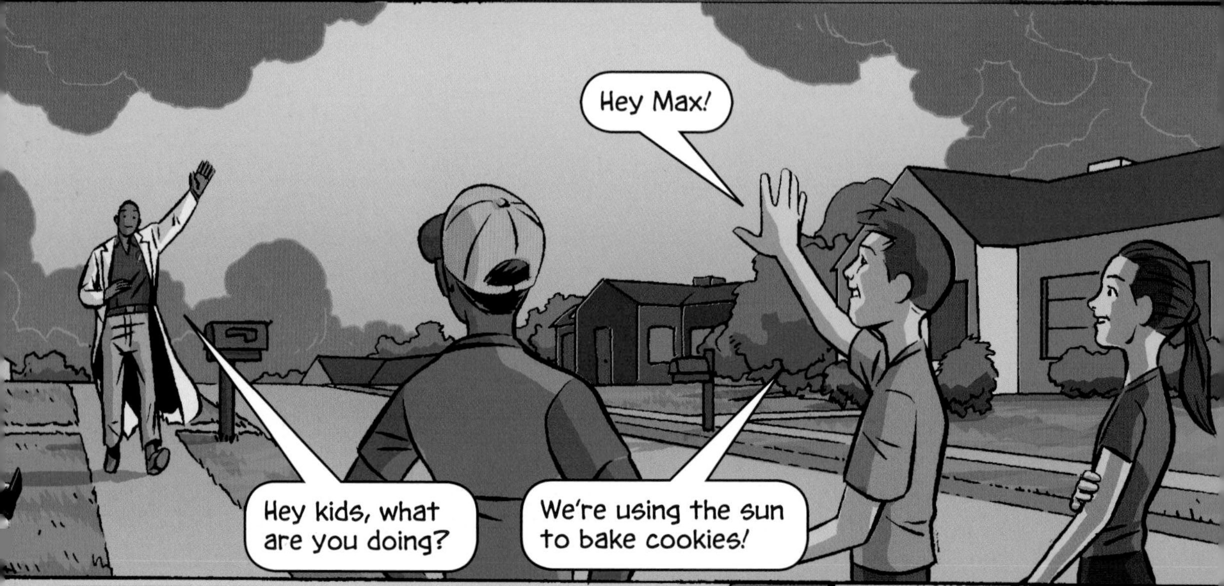
Hey Max!
Hey kids, what are you doing?
We're using the sun to bake cookies!

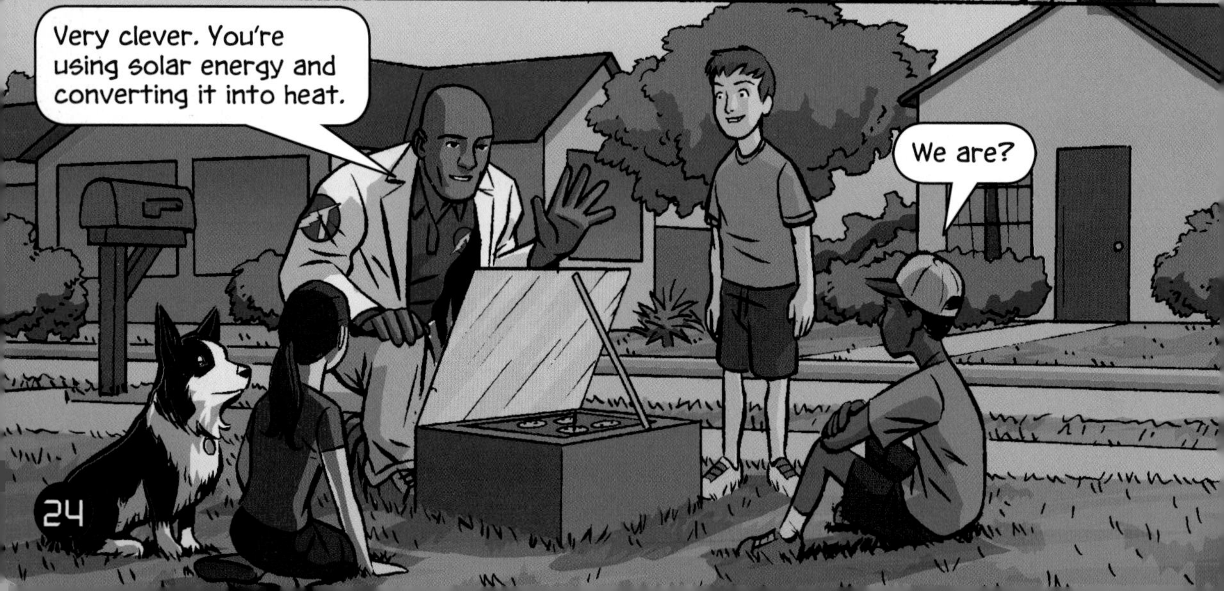
Very clever. You're using solar energy and converting it into heat.
We are?

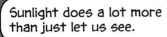

Sunlight does a lot more than just let us see.

Sunlight, or solar energy, can become heat—enough heat to bake cookies in a solar oven.

Thanks for the cookies.

See you later, Max!

SOLAR CELLS

Solar energy can also be changed into electricity.

In fact, some homes collect power with solar cells.

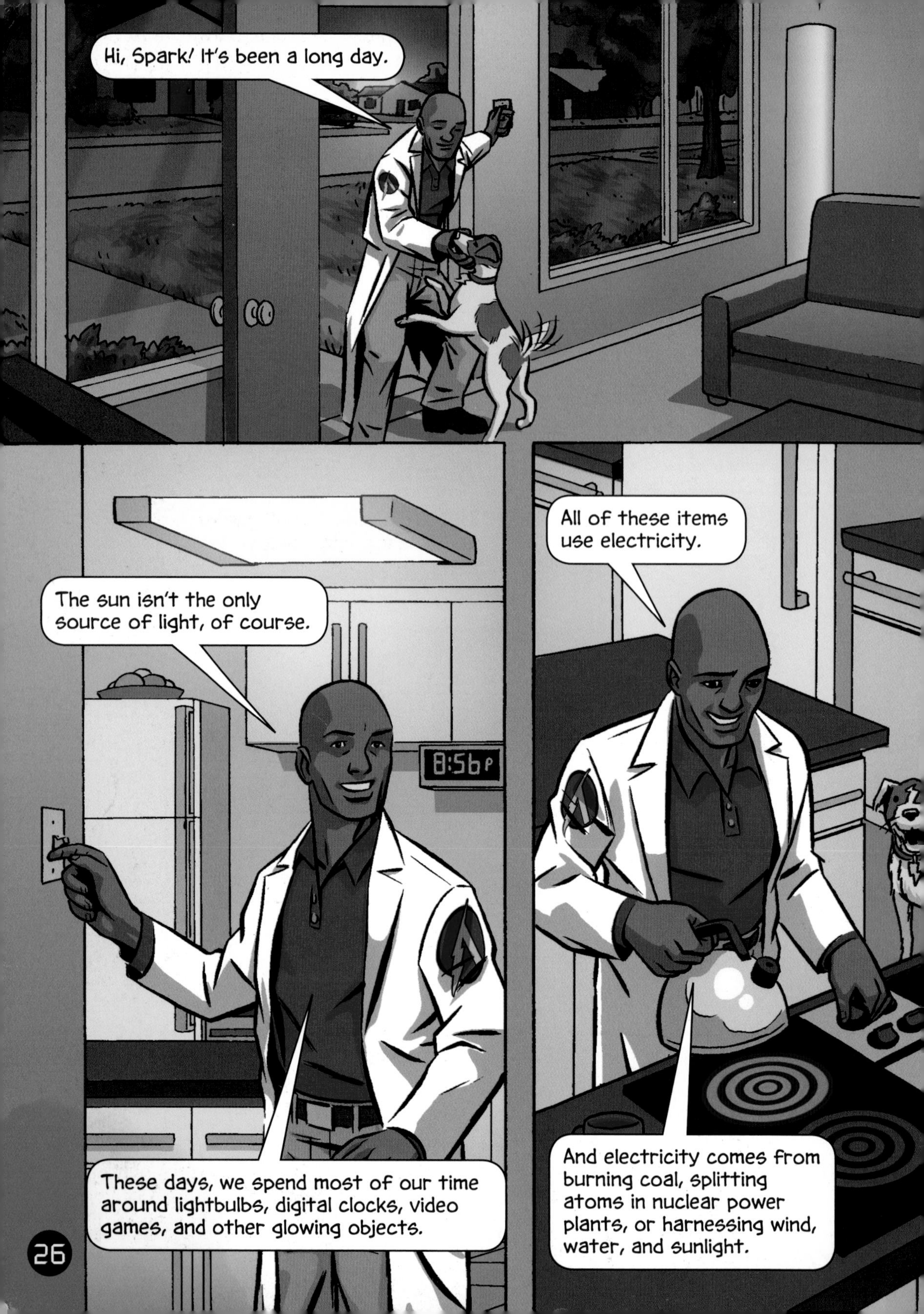
Hi, Spark! It's been a long day.
The sun isn't the only source of light, of course.
8:56 P
These days, we spend most of our time around lightbulbs, digital clocks, video games, and other glowing objects.
All of these items use electricity.
And electricity comes from burning coal, splitting atoms in nuclear power plants, or harnessing wind, water, and sunlight.

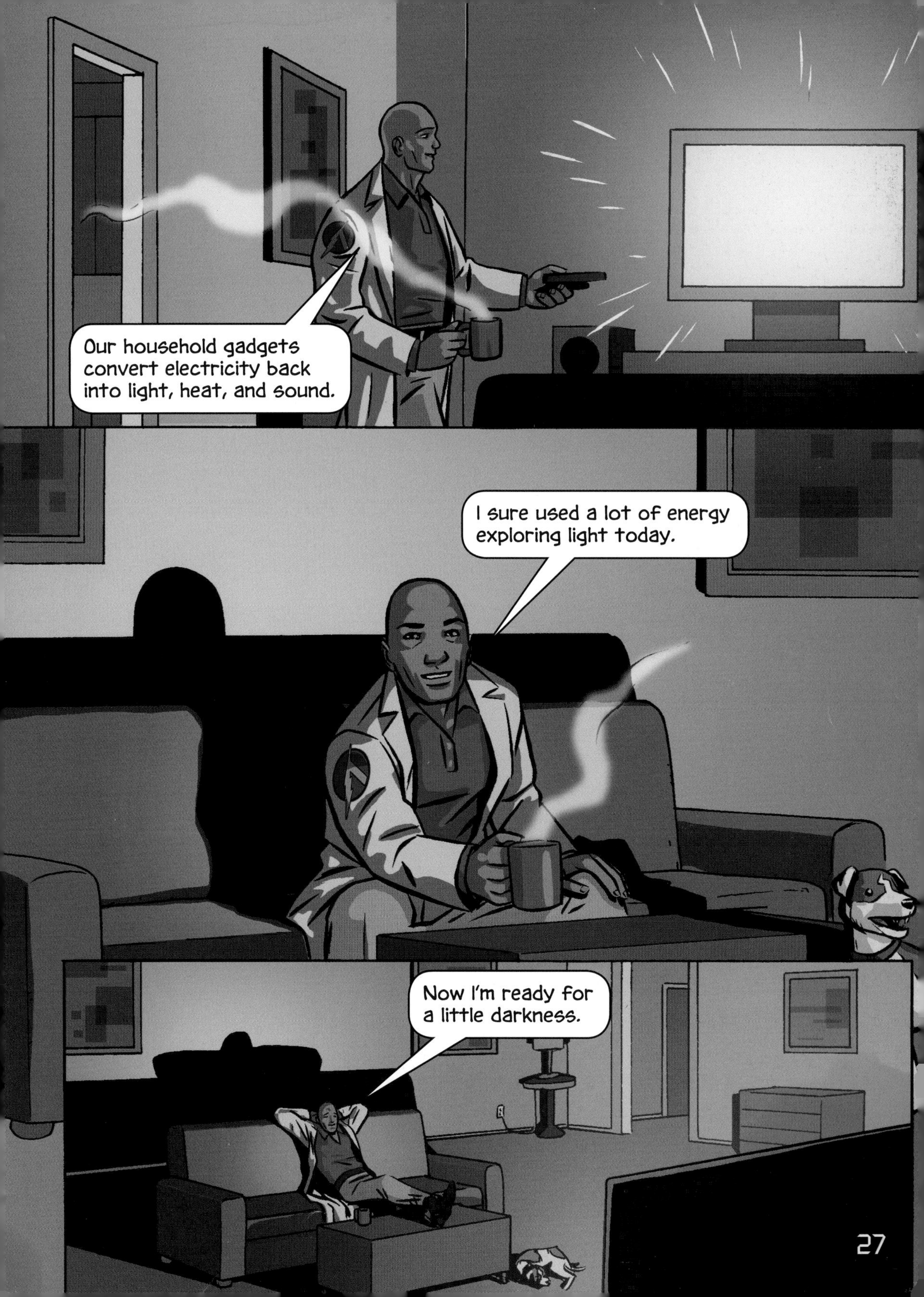
Our household gadgets convert electricity back into light, heat, and sound.
I sure used a lot of energy exploring light today.
Now I'm ready for a little darkness.

MORE ABOUT LIGHT

Light from the sun makes the trip to earth in about 8 minutes and 18 seconds. Traveling the same distance in your car at highway speeds would take more than 170 years.

Light changes speeds when it passes from one material to another. When light passes from air to water, it slows down to about 139,800 miles (225,000 kilometers) per second.

The color of your T-shirt on a sunny, summer day can make a big difference in how hot you feel. Darker colors absorb more light than lighter colors. To stay cooler, wear a white T-shirt on a sunny day because it reflects more light than a darker shirt.

Only 10 percent of the energy used by a regular incandescent lightbulb is changed into visible light. The rest of the energy is wasted as heat.

Telescopes use lenses or mirrors to capture the little bits of light that come to earth from stars, planets, and galaxies in space. The Hubble Space Telescope has allowed us to see galaxies more than 12 billion light-years away.

Human eyes can sense light only within the visible wavelengths on the electromagnetic spectrum. Some animals see the world in a completely different way. Rattlesnakes have sensory pits that detect infrared light. Bees see ultraviolet light.

Moonbows are rainbows that form at night. These faint rainbows form when raindrops refract light reflecting off the moon. When moonlight refracts off ice crystals in the atmosphere, bright halos called moon dogs form around the moon.

Solar energy powers satellites and spacecraft orbiting earth. The International Space Station's huge solar panels turn sunlight into electricity, light, and heat for the astronauts living and working on the spacecraft.

MORE ABOUT

SUPER SCIENTIST

Real name: Maxwell J. Axiom
Hometown: Seattle, Washington
Height: 6' 1"   Weight: 192 lbs
Eyes: Brown   Hair: None

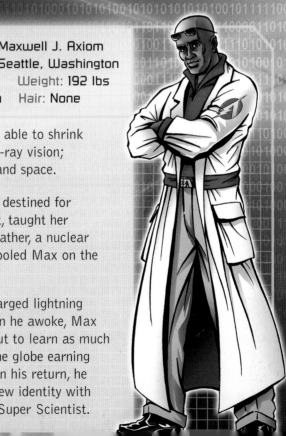

Super capabilities: Super intelligence; able to shrink to the size of an atom; sunglasses give x-ray vision; lab coat allows for travel through time and space.

Origin: Since birth, Max Axiom seemed destined for greatness. His mother, a marine biologist, taught her son about the mysteries of the sea. His father, a nuclear physicist and volunteer park ranger, schooled Max on the wonders of earth and sky.

One day on a wilderness hike, a megacharged lightning bolt struck Max with blinding fury. When he awoke, Max discovered a newfound energy and set out to learn as much about science as possible. He traveled the globe earning degrees in every aspect of the field. Upon his return, he was ready to share his knowledge and new identity with the world. He had become Max Axiom, Super Scientist.

GLOSSARY

atom (AT-uhm)—an element in its smallest form

concave (kahn-KAYV)—hollow and curved, like the inside of a bowl

convex (kahn-VEKS)—curved outward, like the outside of a ball

energy (EN-ur-jee)—the ability to do work, such as moving things or giving heat or light

fusion (FYOO-zhuhn)—the joining together of objects caused by heating; the sun creates its energy with the process of fusion.

infrared light (IN-fruh-red LITE)—light that produces heat; humans cannot see infrared light.

laser (LAY-zur)—a thin, intense, high-energy beam of light

opaque (oh-PAKE)—blocking light

reflection (ree-FLEK-shuhn)—the change in direction of light bouncing off a surface

refract (ree-FRACT)—to bend light as it passes through a substance at an angle

translucent (trans-LOO-suhnt)—letting light pass through, but not transparent; frosted and stained glass are translucent.

transparent (transs-PAIR-uhnt)—letting light through

ultraviolet light (uhl-truh-VYE-uh-lit LITE)—an invisible form of light that can cause sunburns

wavelength (WAYV-length)—the distances between two peaks of a wave

READ MORE

Cooper, Christopher. *Light: From Sun to Bulbs.* Science Answers. Chicago: Heinemann, 2004.

Hamilton, Gina L. *Light: Prisms, Rainbows, and Colors.* Science at Work. Chicago: Raintree, 2004.

Juettner, Bonnie. *Light.* The Kidhaven Science Library. San Diego: Kidhaven Press, 2004.

Lilly, Melinda. *Me and My Shadow.* Read and Do Science. Vero Beach, Fla.: Rourke, 2006.

Richardson, Adele. *Light: A Question and Answer Book.* Questions and Answers: Physical Science. Mankato, Minn.: Capstone Press, 2006.

INTERNET SITES

FactHound offers a safe, fun way to find Internet sites related to this book. All of the sites on FactHound have been researched by our staff.

Here's how:
1. Visit *www.facthound.com*
2. Choose your grade level.
3. Type in this book ID **142960140X** for age-appropriate sites. You may also browse subjects by clicking on letters, or by clicking on pictures and words.
4. Click on the **Fetch It** button.

FactHound will fetch the best sites for you!

INDEX